Furred and Feathered Friends

Also by Richard Inwood and published by Ginninderra Press
The Wandering Albatross

Richard Inwood

Furred and Feathered Friends

Furred and Feathered Friends
ISBN 978 1 76109 411 8
Copyright © text Richard Inwood 2022
Cover painting and design: Annette Inwood

First published 2022 by
Ginninderra Press
PO Box 3461 Port Adelaide 5015
www.ginninderrapress.com.au

Introduction

As English children in India, my brothers, sisters and I were products of an era now past. We were in tune with the country and fluent in the language. It was paradise for a boy. Shooting and fishing were our sport. We were never teenagers in the modern, contemporary sense, and all the awkwardness and other facets of the growing-up period were effectively modified in swamps and jungle terrain, shotgun blasts and concentrating on a truer aim.

Roaming the countryside was a learning experience: accepting the friendship of villagers, eating the offered unleavened bread, and slaking our thirst with fresh sugar cane juice. We passed on news of the outside world and learnt the movement of game from them. We preferred village people to the city and bazaar dwellers, because of the simple, honest and down to earth philosophy of their way of life.

We progressed from slingshots to airguns, .22 rifles, single- and double-barrelled shotguns, and on to more sophisticated heavy weaponry for wild boar and bigger game. A box of three-inch Eley Alphamax number eight chilled shot for use in a shotgun was handled with the reverence normally reserved for the Bible.

Squirrels on high branches were not safe, nor were doves on telegraph wires. Egrets were erased off buffalos' backs. Hawks and crows took cover. We were gun-happy.

I make no excuses, except to say it was an established way of life. Wildlife was abundant and we ate what we shot. Blue rock pigeons, mallard, pintail, pochard and teal made excellent curries and stews. With black buck and cheetal deer, the rule was to avoid shooting the female. The hides were treated and tanned and used to make our shoes and boots. Only one egg was to be taken from a nest. My father would not tolerate unnecessary cruelty and believed in quick dispatch. My mother never ceased to remonstrate and, when coercion of all kinds failed, would resort to the fear of God. Some of my earliest memories are of her saying, 'God will punish you for this,' as a broken, wounded bird lay in the palm of her hand. It still haunts me.

However, we did have wild creatures as pets, on whom we'd lavish care and affection. My favourite was a deer named Bessie, with the softest brown eyes you've ever seen. She'd daintily tiptoe into the house to have her ears rubbed. Two peacocks and nine peahens roamed in our backyard. We hatched partridge eggs under our bantam hens; the babies were fed on white ants and when mature we released them into the countryside. Bulbuls and mynah birds flew around the house. We brought home wounded wild ducks and treated them with loving care, housed them in a separate area simulating a swamp, and when they were recovered, we released them. Bullock cart drivers who mistreated their animals while hauling their loads received a number of slugs from our favourite airguns.

No domestic fowl or duck could be had for dinner. When our mother decided to have fowl for dinner, it had to be whispered to our cook, Abdul, when we were out of earshot. When we did find out, Abdul would pay the penalty. He was a Moslem and it was an incumbent religious belief for him to cut their throats, while uttering, 'Bismillah, Allah I'll Allah.' It horrified us.

We'd set up a small home-made cannon, primed with a small charge of gunpowder, a wad, a teaspoon of dust shot and a short fuse. We'd call him and as he waddled out of his kitchen, framed in the doorway, he'd receive a charge on his ample belly, enough to make him scratch. Yet he loved us as we loved him. He was with our family for thirty years.

It was a good boyhood, though some would disagree. We were boys, omnipotent with the power of life and death, but we were at a crossroads, uncertain of the path to follow. Maturity brought a modicum of wisdom and with it were feelings of regret, and the need to change.

After many years of wandering, I came to Australia. In 1961, I met a young girl, Annette. We fell in love and got married. Under her influence, I travelled down the road to a new way of life. This book describes the journey.

1

My family left India in early 1948 after independence was achieved, forming part of a massive diaspora during which thousands set sail for England, Australia, Canada and other destinations. From hot dusty plains to the soft greens of the English countryside. We had to adapt to a different lifestyle, embrace the new culture, find work and start our careers.

I went to a radio college and joined the British Merchant Navy in 1949 as a radio officer, subsequently spending eleven years at sea. The first year was on ships crossing the English Channel, often in treacherous weather, Dover to Dunkirk, Folkestone to Boulogne, Southampton to the Channel Islands, then five years on the China coast with the China Navigation Company, followed by a return to the UK for further study and then five years on a Greek tanker, tramping around the oceans of the world but mainly around South America.

I left the sea in 1960. After eleven years looking at distant horizons, I realised that in all that time I'd only spent seven months at home. I was thirty-one years of age and I was ready for a new life. Radio static and the throb of the engines were a constant in my life. I signed off in Philadelphia, went down to Florida to see my brother, who lived in Fort Lauderdale, to say goodbye, was repatriated to England and shortly after sailed out to Sydney, where my parents and another brother had settled.

I found work immediately as a radio officer with the Overseas Telecommunications Commission. I lived in Manly, as a lone ex-mariner. One day from my upstairs flat I saw a young girl on the lawn below, lying on a beach towel in bathers under a magnolia tree, reading a book. She was lovely.

I screwed up enough courage to consider approaching her to have a chat, Despite more than a decade of wandering worldwide, and meeting and talking to people, I was no longer the shy young virgin of nineteen who had left India for the UK. I'd had eleven years at sea since then. Experienced seafarers had taken me under their wing, and in various ports of the world I'd met women who provided comfort, warmth and fun. Here on Australian soil, a newcomer, I felt somewhat unsure of how to conduct myself.

I approached her tentatively and said, 'Hello.'

She looked up. A pretty brunette, with blue-green eyes. I guessed about twenty years of age. With a swift glance, I saw that she was reading Gerald Durrell's *My family and Other Animals*.

'A good book?' I ventured. I paused and then added, 'I have an interest in animals.'

'Yes?' she raised her eyebrows.

I wondered if it was just an expression, or a question for me to explain. 'I was born in India. We grew up with pets, wild birds, peafowl, even a deer.'

She put her book down and sat up.

'I'm sorry... I've interrupted your reading,' I said.

She shook her head. 'I've just come to the end of a chapter.' She paused. 'May I ask what you're doing here?' She let the question hang. 'Us girls in the flat below often wonder. We see you driving around during the day with a fishing rod between the seats.'

I smiled. 'Ah well,. I work at a maritime radio station, mostly at nights, down at La Perouse. I was a radio officer at sea for many years. I only came ashore a few months ago.' I laughed. 'I just remembered that my best friend, my companion, was a canary called Jimmy. We were together on a Greek tanker for five years. I still miss him. My interest in animals and birds is based on my upbringing in India.'

She raised her eyebrows and seemed to be interested but said nothing. She was shy, I guess. I was silent for a while and then on an impulse I apologised for disturbing her. She smiled and said that it was fine. Later, much later, she confided in me saying that she could see the loneliness in my eyes. That I was somewhat lost, and friendless.

2

Not long after that meeting, I went for a stroll, feeling somewhat restless. Life on the high seas was over. A life on land lay ahead of me. Thinking like a mariner, I felt that this was it, the final port. Engines stopped. At anchor.

A factor that gave me some comfort was that at Sydneyradio I was working with a cosmopolitan group. Sixteen Australians, fifteen British, three Dutch, two Italians, three Scandanavians, one Greek and one Lebanese, reflecting quite accurately the national proportions. All were products of differing environments and when we came together on a shift, we were all aware that we had an affinity with the sea, the common bond. We were also aware that the Mediterranean group would on occasions fill the canteen with the stench of garlic, rank goat's milk cheese and scattered seeds from kalimata olives, causing mainly good-humoured protest. The average age was in the region of forty years. All were radio officers who had served in the merchant fleets of their respective nations. All had the benefits of travel, tolerance and a facility in foreign tongues.

We had an important role. Every ship that entered or left this harbour used us as a link. Morse code was our language. We'd pick them up weeks away and usher them in, and when they sailed, we'd follow them to their destinations. A British tanker with blistering decks coming out of the Persian Gulf is given its discharge orders. A Russian from the cold fog off Vladivostock is told where to pick up his cargo of wheat, a Japanese ore carrier wallowing in a low pressure area sends a weather report, and a liner just leaving Southampton calls to say he's on his way.

Our main role of course was the 'safety of life at sea' – SOLAS. A twenty-four-hour watch on the calling and distress frequency of

500khz, a vital link in the search and rescue organisation worldwide. All of us were aware of the perils of life at sea, the mountains of foam flecked green, screeching winds, hove to and riding out the storm.

I was sitting on a slatted bench near Manly Wharf watching the locals try their luck with the flathead and bream. Hoots and shouts. The ferries coming in, blue water and red-roofed houses, and ships going through the Heads, as I had so many times, looking shorewards and knowing I'd be back. Australia in the 1960s was a brave new land with a future and a vibrant population. I'd always carried the picture of George Street full of bright, summer dresses worn by suntanned girls.

I was content. The sun was comfortable and I began to feel drowsy, locked in an introspective shell, barely aware of the bustle of ferries coming and going, and the crowds of hurrying people. I was not yet a part of them. I was a stranger, or a distant relative looking for a family to fit into. I'd been wandering too long, searching for a home. The words of a poem came to me. How did it go?

> The restless thrill of changing skies. Only for him who knows the ceaseless urge to go, go ever on, carried by the tide and trade winds pulsing surge, lured by the bright mirage of far off places, forests and jungles and bleak frozen places.

I thought of the girl I'd talked to a week ago. I'd enjoyed our chat. I eased myself on the bench and closed my eyes. My adolescent years and those of this girl were a decade apart. Born in different hemispheres, the only thing we had in common was an interest in animals, just a flimsy link, but nevertheless it was enough to give me hope.

It wasn't too long ago I was a young lad on the Indian plains, a schoolboy up in the Himalayas, sure-footed as a mountain goat. Only a dog watch ago, I was on the wing of a bridge, watching the bow rise and fall, punching into a force seven Atlantic gale. Florida and airboat rides. Fishing for tarpon and amberjack in the Everglades. Across the Atlantic, New York to Southampton and then out to Australia.

I sat quietly watching the sun begin its descent and the first chill of the evening came on. I was barely aware of the increased rush hour activity on the wharf as people returned, hurrying from the city.

I saw the girl as she turned onto the footpath.

She stepped off the path and paused. 'Hello,' she said.

Instinctively, I shuffled to give her space.

She sat beside me. 'You seemed to be far away,' she said.

'Yes, I was,' I replied, 'remembering things. It's nice here.'

'Do you come here often?'

'First time, really.' I looked at her and smiled. 'I have a day off, so I thought I'd see how the fishing is. What bait to use. Learn from the experts.'

'And did you?'

'Yes, but no one ever lets a fish go. They're just hauled up and left to gasp their lives away. In England, in the ponds and lakes where you pay a few shillings, a fish is caught, handled gently, admired and released.'

She looked at me, intrigued. It was something she'd never heard of. Such a caring tradition. She obviously hated cruelty to animals. It was probably why she liked Durrell's books so much.

'I've just bought a rod,' I continued, 'but I don't think I'll be using it a lot.'

She was quiet for a few seconds. 'We thought you were an American. That slight accent, and you have a nice Holden. We even thought you could be a rich American,' she smiled.

'Sorry,' he laughed. 'Yes, when I was at sea I spent quite some time on the American coasts. No, I was born in India.'

'More surprises,' she laughed. 'I've always been fascinated by those places. India, China, the Far East. India, millions of people, heat, snakes and things that crawl. I suppose you've seen snake charmers and cobras?' She pronounced it like cob, as in Bob, or corn on the cob. I corrected her quietly. 'Not cob. It should rhyme with cove. Like cove-ra. Cobra. Yes, I've seen them. One struck at me once.'

She looked at me closely. 'How? How did it happen?'

'Well, it's a long story.' I paused. 'It's getting cool. Would you like to go for a drive? Could you show me the way to Long Reef?'

'It's just up the road. That would be nice, as long as I'm home by six.'

We walked up the Corso and into Darley Road to where my car was parked. My first car, an FJ Holden.

'Sorry about the fishing rod,' I said.

It was in the middle of the front bench seat, pointing down to the floorboards and up over the seat, almost touching the roof.

It was beautiful at Long Reef, looking down on the sea just as the sun began to set. Far out a tanker was heading south. I talked all about the sea and my experiences. She listened intently, her body turned towards me.

I paused. 'Perhaps I'm talking too much. I haven't talked so much for a long time.' I looked into her face and into her green eyes.

'I'm listening,' she said, 'but you're going too fast. So many things I know so little about. I don't want to miss anything. Tell me about the cobra.'

'Well, it's not much,' I said.

I liked this girl. I felt good about her. Wanted her to be a friend. I wanted to tell her things, to sort of open up. I hoped that she liked me. Nineteen, twenty maybe, a lovely face. Petite. We seemed natural together, despite the age difference. I smiled to myself.

'Why? Why are you smiling?' she said.

'Happy, I guess.' I cleared my throat. 'Well, this cobra,' and I began to laugh.

'Now what?' she said.

I shook my head. 'Here we are. A thousand things to say. This scene in front of us, that tanker out there, engines throbbing. I could be on the bridge. Snakes, how did we get onto snakes? On that bench near the ferry, I was thinking how it all works out, how paths are set for us to follow. I'm a stranger here, haven't lived ashore for eleven years, still thinking of port and starboard and yet, here we are.'

She seemed to want to reach out and touch my face in sympathy. Instead, she narrowed her eyes in mock impatience. 'Are you going to tell me about this snake or not?'

'Well, this was in northern India, north-east of Delhi, a small place called Saharanpur. I was about sixteen at the time. We were having lunch and heard a commotion outside. Indians are quite excitable. A mob of them were on the veranda, all talking at once. Evidently, a cobra had been disturbed in a field by a shepherd and his cattle. The cattle had stampeded, causing the cobra to cross the road, pursued by a crowd throwing stones and clods of earth. It had entered a guava orchard and gone into a small hut in which the chowkidar or watchman lived. He was in there, trapped, hanging onto the bars of the window and screaming his head off. It was very big, they said. "Better take the gun and have a look," my dad said.

'I picked up the old long-barrelled Midland 12-gauge shotgun and a couple of number eight cartridges. Not a gun for close-range work. I could hear the fellow shrieking from a long way off. The people outside were hurling stones and let out a cheer as I came up. The door swung inwards and the snake was behind it. There was no other way but to go in. I fed the cartridges into the gun and pulled the hammers back. I flattened myself against the door jamb and quietly entered the doorway, knowing the cobra had sensed me come in.

'The crowd was silent now, holding its breath. I know I was. I took a step in. The door was still in between us. I leaned to one side and looked at the snake. It was big, it was ready and as I moved one step further, there it was, poised to strike, a quarter of its length raised, slanted upwards from its coiled base with the head half a metre off the ground. It was all of two metres long and there was just half that distance between us. I knew that the shot would come out like a solid ball. I froze. The snake spread its hood and arched its back in a sort of sinuous motion. It swayed back and forth, beady eyes glaring, decreasing and increasing its height and making puffing sounds. I felt cold all over. I thought to myself that if it struck, even with my finger on the trigger I wouldn't have time to pull. I stayed still, fascinated by the thin forked tongue speeding in and out from its lips. I had to get out of striking range.

'The snake seemed to cool down a bit and slowly lowered itself and then bumped its nostrils against a crack in the door, scenting the air outside. There was no escape for it and for a moment I felt sorry. I took one big stride away and in a flash it struck at the last movement of my shoes, unbelievably fast. I felt it slam against my heel in a sort of deflected strike that sent its head against the cement. You should have seen it then. It reared back, spread its hood and the coils made a quick muscular adjustment and up he rose making hissing sounds. My heart was racing. The crowd outside had seen the strike and let go a yell. The big stride I'd made put me far enough across the room, out of his range, and I had room to fire. Very slowly, I brought the gun up and he increased his height as if planning a long strike. I froze for about ten seconds and brought the gun up to my shoulder, and as I expected, he came up following the muzzle, directly in front, and I pulled the trigger. Well, that's the story.'

She looked at me, her eyes scanning my face as though searching for the boy of my past. 'What a different life you've had.' She could see it all in her mind, transported there and looking into a cube that was a room, a figure, a gun, a snake and then a bang in her ears. She had tears in her eyes. 'Poor thing,' she said. 'Deadly but the way you described it, so brave and fearless. I can imagine it saying to you, "Stand back. No closer or I'll strike. I'm warning you."' She blinked and gave an embarrassed laugh. She dug for a tissue in her handbag.

'I'm sorry,' I said. In telling the story, I could feel himself reliving it, his senses alert and tingling. I reached out and touched her arm. 'Sorry,' I repeated.

She looked at me, searching for the softness in my face reflecting my inner feelings. 'I just felt so sorry,' she said. There was a sheen in her eyes.

I nodded. 'I feel sorry too. What right did I have to blow its head off? A thing like that, perfect, in its prime. It wasn't its fault. It was provoked. Oh, they were patting me on the back, I was a brave young sahib and all that. I did what was expected. In India, if you see a snake and have a gun, you shoot it. That's the only excuse I have. The mob took it outside, chucked it around, jumped on it, yelling and laughing.'

There was a long pause.

'I can imagine you there. I'd love to go to India. It would be fascinating,' she said.

'For a girl alone, it would be dangerous. Let me know and I'll come with you,' I smiled.

I looked at her and I knew that I could love this woman and live with her. I was in love. It was founded on a strong base of mutual affinity and respect for animals, domestic and wild, the latter more predominant in my case.

We poured our hearts out. I told her about my boyhood. Because of the oppressive heat down in the Indian plains, all European children were sent to school up in the Himalayan foothills, where we'd spend nine months, followed by three months back with our parents when it was cooler. When in school, it was quite common to see black bears on the hills opposite, leopards on the hockey field and hear the thump as they jumped onto the metal corridors that connected the school buildings. Black-faced monkeys, langurs, were everywhere and invariably we'd have fights with them using our slingshots. They were fearless and keen to do battle. We knew the calls of birds and at night in our beds we'd hear the bark of a barking deer, a muntjac, and the rasping cough of a leopard on the prowl.

Boys will be boys. We'd catch relatively harmless grass snakes and keep them in our pockets, feeding them with bread soaked in milk. I had a couple and used them to good effect when we'd meet the girls from our sister school, who'd file into one side and we on the other when we met at church. There was the usual giggling, flirting and coy looks and I'd choose the right moment during the singing or kneeling to pray to slide a snake across the aisle. Mayhem! Alternatively, at a school fete a writhing snake inserted into a huddle of girls caused quite a stir.

I learnt that she had been raised in Sydney, a Lane Cove girl. She used to dress her father's hens in dolls clothes and wheel them around in a doll's pram. The hapless fowls actually got used to it and would doze quietly. She also described a long line of cats and dogs, including one called Lassie that would escort her as a young teenager diligently on a thirty-minute walk to the railway station, then scuttle home fast to report to her mother, wagging her tail and rump indicating a successful mission. Lassie also had a series of barks, low- and high-pitched, the latter being used to alert Annette's mum that local children were throwing stones at her. Then there was a canary, Goldie, who was better than an alarm clock. She would exit her permanently open cage, sweep low over the recumbent forms of her humans, fanning their faces to wake them up. Actually, she wanted the sugar bowl filled on the table.

Over the next few weeks, we drew closer and closer together. One evening, Annette climbed the stairs to my room upstairs carefully carrying an unwanted kitten. The girls she shared the downstairs flat with had told her to get rid of it.

I looked at it cupped protectively in her hands. 'Poor little sod,' I said. 'Where can we keep it?' Our first pet.

She lifted her eyes to mine and we knew we were soulmates. We met regularly and went for drives, once to a movie and once to a restaurant.

She took me to the Wenona Tuck Shop to meet her mother, Eva, and we got on fine. I took her to see Mum, Dad and brother Ed and his family. They were delighted with her, and Dad tried to put a pinch of snuff up her nose. He was a bit of a flirt. I was the long lost youngest son, home to roost, and hopefully we'd have a son in due course. Ed had two girls, and my other brothers were childless. I knew Annette's mother approved of me but I had to pass muster with her father. We met in the lounge room of their house in Lane Cove and had a chat over a shot of whisky. I assured him I was unmarried and had a couple of thousand quid. I didn't tell him that I'd blown thousands all over the world.

One good thing about working at Sydneyradio was that the manager was quite tolerant and allowed us to bring our female friends to the station, occasionally. I was on the 16mhz console sending and receiving messages, giving Annette an idea of what went on.

Ken, the manager came over and said, 'Dick, head office wants to send a good man up to Port Moresby and I've recommended you. What d'you think?'

'When, Ken?'

'About a month. A bloke has to go to Rabaul, which is short-staffed, and you'll take his place.'

'I'll take it. I was on that run when I was with China Nav way back in '52, on the *Soochow*.' I turned to Annette and said, 'You'll come with me, won't you?'

She laughed. 'Is this a proposal of marriage?'

'Er,' I was momentarily speechless. Then I blurted out, 'Yes, of course. Will you marry me?'

'Yes, I will, of course,' she laughed happily.

We'd known each other for three weeks.

Ken immediately congratulated us. 'I'm a witness. Very unexpected. Well, I'll tell HO. A month – doesn't give you much time.'

It was somewhat of a blur after that. Parents to be told, and friends. Wedding arrangements to make. The church and the reception venue to be arranged. A new suit for me and wedding gear for Annette.

It all worked out fine. Annette was a beautiful bride. To this day, I do not recall what I said in my speech. I know I was terrified. Annette held my hand under the tablecloth. We had a whirlwind honeymoon in the New South Wales highlands, and the company kindly gave us a couple of extra weeks, allowing us a leisurely voyage up to Moresby on the *Bulolo*. Nine years in Papua New Guinea followed.

3

We had been living in Port Moresby for only a month or so when we found our first homeless creature.

I was driving home to our house on Ela Beach. It was an old place, built up a slope on a foundation of large rocks, an ideal spot for the snakes that inhabited the area. Formerly a radio station, it had been damaged during the war and rebuilt. Quite comfortable. Located in an ideal spot right on the corner where Musgrave Street curved down to Ela Beach. From our bedroom, we could see the palm trees swaying, hear the lap of waves and best of all, feel the cool sea breeze.

I was on my way back home from Jackson's airstrip, coming down Three-mile Hill. It was one of those cool, tropical evenings that brought relief from the glaring heat of Moresby's dry season. I felt compelled to pull over to a lookout point to admire the view. It was beautiful. I was overlooking dense green vegetation stretching down to Badili, and on to the palm trees rising from Koki Market. Then the sea, blue and calm out to the main reef, with lonely Basilisk Beacon marking the entrance. Someone out there was doing figure of eights, trolling for tuna and a fleet of lakatois were tacking their way back to Koki.

A Papuan boy came down the road holding a featherless squab of a bird in his hand. I called out, a bit concerned to see it was attached to his wrist by a thin piece of wire around its leg. When he approached, I examined the bird. At least sixty per cent of its body was featherless and the rest, particularly the wings, was covered with a blue-white stubble of pin feathers. Its eyes were closed and the well-defined yellow strip around the mouth was zippered tight. I imagined that when grown it would it would be the size of a thrush, although I doubted the poor thing would live that long.

I didn't think that the boy knew the name of the bird, but I asked anyway. 'Nem bilong 'im?

'The boy rubbed his feet together and thought for a moment. 'Manu,' he replied.

Later I was to learn that manu is the name for all birds.

I had some loose change in my jacket pocket and put all the coins in the palm of my hand. 'Wan silling, tu silling?' I said and waited.

Behind furrowed brows the boy deliberated, unhurriedly working out a price. I was to learn later that the price of a bird or animal related to the value placed on its meat in the market place.

'Two silling,' he eventually replied.

I gave him the money, and an extra shilling, and took the bird. I was rewarded with a big smile, revealing white teeth yet unstained by betel nut juice.

I put the orphan deep inside a string bag, locally known as a bilum, in which my lunch box, tobacco, pipes and other oddments were carried, and drove on homewards. Possession of the hapless thing was enough to make me feel like a boy scout who'd accomplished his good deed for the day. Optimistically, I could foresee no problems except the immediate one of cleaning the green-white deposit on my lunch box, which the bird in a purely functional and uninterested way had placed there with a tiny squirt of sound. At least its bowels were not bound. White was calcium and green would be chlorophyll from vegetable matter.

I was considering the whole business when I got home and was met by Annette. She gave a little shriek when I produced the bird, a mixture of surprise, alarm at its naked state and perhaps some inner voicing of her maternal instincts. The moment she placed it in her cupped hand and made a shelter over it with her other hand I knew it would be safe. Baby birds, like human babies, are demanding creatures requiring regular feeds, their messes cleaned, mothering and a warm, sheltered place of their own. This bird had it made.

We had no idea of what sort of bird it was, but we didn't have much time to ponder the problem because no sooner had we revived it with some water from an eye dropper, than it had its yellow mouth wide open, screeching with a peculiarly high-pitched sound we were to hear regularly from then on.

The bird's urgency was accentuated by a shuffling of its featherless, stubby wings, and faced with the incessant demand from this skinny, tiny and tattered piece of nothing, two adults were running towards the kitchen. We found some mince defrosting for the evening meal and, making small parcels, we dropped them one by one into the gaping beak. Each morsel was readily received, and when the mouth remained shut, we realised with relief that he was full, for the moment. We decided that the regular diet would be mince meat, egg and for good measure a few drops of Pentavite, a vitamin mixture for babies. Annette prepared a small box for him and we lifted the dozing bird into it. Because of its dishevelled state, we decided to call him or her Tatters.

Tatters demanded a meal every half hour, so Annette was forced to carry a small cardboard box containing him and his requirements of meat and water everywhere she went, shopping or visiting. Whenever a raucous noise was heard from the box, to the wonderment of Europeans and native Papuans alike, she would lift the lid and feed the bird. For the Papuans, this was altogether something very strange.

Annette took to phoning me at work with reports on Tatters's progress and with reminders to collect grasshoppers from the bush around the communication station. From books at the local library, we found that she was a female fawn-breasted bowerbird. Also from the printed pages, we discovered her dietary requirements which made her omnivorous and I had the task of finding worms, beetles and grasshoppers, in addition to chopping up vegetable matter.

Within a month, Tatters was out of her box and hopping around the house. However, as we had polished floors, she had to exercise some care since any fast hops resulted in a long skid, ending up with her on her bottom.

We had another homeless waif by this time, a part-terrier rescued at six weeks of age, condemned to be destroyed. Her owners were going south, back to Australia. We named her Tanya. It is a natural instinct for a terrier to chase game, but Tanya wished only to please and, responding to firm commands ,soon realised that Tatters was important to us and was another member of the family. Though sorely tempted by Tatters hopping and skipping across the room, she would deliberately turn her head and look the other way, and when the provocation became extreme, she'd resist temptation by removing herself from the room entirely. However, her natural instincts would sometimes come to the fore and she'd issue a warning by showing a curled lip exposing a number of canines and giving a low growl. Tatters soon got the message.

Months later ,Tatters was still completely dependent on Annette and attempts to teach her to feed herself failed. Food would be offered to her in the hand but would be ignored until actually placed in her mouth. Dishes left in her cage with the most succulent morsels would be ignored.

Annette hardened her heart. There was a pitiful period for a couple of days and finally Tatters in desperation made the initial move and took a bite, and another, followed by an onslaught on the tidbits in her dishes. We were very relieved, now satisfied with just being the supplier.

The heat and humidity, and the stubbornness of Tatters and other daily chores, including giving piano lessons every day, were enough to sap Annette's energy but nevertheless, on one particular evening, she responded at once to my urgent call for help when I phoned her. I was in the town office where all Morse and teleprinter traffic was handled. I was in the process of shutting down the communication circuit with Sydney, sending and receiving the last of the day's traffic coming into the Territory. The receptionist who accepted messages at the front office counter, counting the number of words, bundling the forms and sending them down the chute, had gone home and I was alone.

From very scant, tentative press releases down in mainland Australia, this morning, it appeared that a son of Nelson Rockefeller, the American billionaire, was missing in Dutch New Guinea. I assumed the story would all become clear later.

I was looking forward to going home and having a nice cold beer when I heard the sound of voices, heavy treading, coarse language and the movement of bodies coming up the stairs into the front office. I took my earphones off and went to investigate. I was staggered to find as many as ten reporters, most of them unshaven and bedraggled, jostling each other, some with beer bottles, others asking for water and waving their closely typed forms and pushing forward to have their copy sent first. Two of them were mates of mine, both working for Australian press. I saw badges showing *New York Times* and *Washington Post*, the ABC, BBC, *Daily Mail*, Agence France, the German *Zeitung*, Dutch and Belgian papers. There was a cacophony of sound and I was overwhelmed by the task facing me. Aware that they knew the procedure, I took the forms from my mate, knowing that they would have paged their copy into fifty-word groups with a line between each group, making it easy to count the total.

Looking at this mob, I anticipated having to send about fifteen thousand words and no way in the world could I prepare, count and collate that amount and then send the whole lot down to Sydney on my own. I called out that I'd handle the situation but I needed help, and picked up the phone to ring the manager. There was no answer, nor from the receptionist. In the meantime, some of them had gone into the operating room and were drinking from the tap above the sink there, and others I could see were getting restive.

Above the babble, I began to piece the story together. It seemed that Michael Rockefeller, son of the famous family, had disappeared in the area inhabited by the Asmat people in Dutch New Guinea. They were a primitive tribe only recently contacted by missionaries. They had been until recently at the cannibal stage. They were renowned for their wood carving skills throughout the Pacific region, creating primitive motifs and totem poles, features well known to Rockefeller, who on previous occasions had risked entry into their area, with guides, acquiring priceless pieces for display in the Metropolitan Museum of Art in New York. They lived in an extremely remote area in a vast tangled area of jungle, crocodile-infested rivers and mangrove swamps, providing rich natural resources, fish and forest game. The nearest town, Merauke, was a hundred miles away.

American, Australian and Dutch resources were being used to search the area and the Rockefeller family were using their wealth to assist in any way possible. It had gained worldwide attention and the reports were that his craft had been swept down the river, out into the open sea with a disabled engine and drifting further away from the shore, which was about four kilometres distant. It was speculated that he had decided to swim to the coast, ignoring the urgings of his companion not to do so. He vanished and the assumption was that he had been taken by a shark or saltwater crocodile.

The world press had descended on Merauke, where the communications facilities were minimal, with a similar dearth of stores, accommodation and general infrastructure. The reporters had boarded a motley collection of light planes and headed for Port Moresby, and here they were.

I made many calls to the manager and got no response. Our house was next door to his, so I asked Annette to go across. She found no one there. It was then that I told her my plight and asked her to come over as soon as possible. When she came, she too was overwhelmed by the presence of these men, all of them news hounds and somewhat aggressive in nature. I gave her a quick course in word counting, paging into fifty-word groups, putting the office of origin at the top of the form, date and time and word count and cost involved.

Having previously worked in a bank, nimble with figures and with a keen mind, she began her work while I went back into the operating room, gave Sydney the news that a pile of traffic was coming and to keep the circuit open. Copy after copy came down the chute and I began my transmissions, on and on and on. We didn't finish until midnight and were totally exhausted.

It was quite an experience for both of us. Years later, a book was published by an author whom I met at a writers festival. He had gone back into the Asmat area, talking to the elders and gradually learning their secrets. His exhaustive research revealed that in fact Michael Rockefeller had been killed by the Asmats, ritually dismembered and eaten. The press interest faded. None of them felt the urge to do further investigation, entering dangerous areas. They left it to the intrepid author who ventured into hostile country. He certainly deserved the credit.

After that episode, life went back to normal. Tatters now had her full plumage and was about nine inches in length, from top of beak to end of tail: the size of a dove but far more slender and with longer legs. She could take to the air but preferred to move from room to room with a brief aerial bounce, a hop, skip and jump. Our long back veranda was a perfect aviary, completely enclosed by cyclone wire mesh, and it provided her with ample room for exercise as it ran the full length of the house.

Though closely related to birds of paradise and a descendant of common stock, she was at the end of the queue when the supply of exotic colours ran out and was relegated to the role of a drab country cousin. However, Nature had ensured that her soft, fawn-coloured breast feathers, merging delicately with light chocolate-coloured wings, dotted with grey-white specks, would provide perfect camouflage for her low bush- and ground-dwelling role.

To us, she was beautiful and her soft, liquid-brown eyes were her best feature. Friends who came to visit us could see none of these attributes, much to our disappointment, and I think we were considered rather odd when we talked about her as a person, or as a child whom we scolded for being naughty. I was especially fascinated by the facility she possessed of being able to face one way and with absolute ease twist her neck so that she was looking straight over the centre line of her back, remarkable in that she didn't have a long neck, but even this inherent skill failed to arouse comment. I was convinced that through the aeons of evolutionary time this flexibility had been acquired either for survival or courtship purposes.

Annette was particularly able to eulogise on her intelligence and other merits, to which the bird listened approvingly, canting her head this way and that to catch each syllable and inflection, shuffling her wings as her mother lapsed into little nothings of baby talk, which I'm sure the guests found disconcerting. I sat by, concerned with more practical matters, pockets stuffed with convenient sizes of toilet paper, springing into action when I saw a telltale mark on the polished floor.

Tatters didn't have her spacious veranda to herself for very long. On one of our exploratory drives around Moresby, we found a small private zoo and acquired another bird. The place was run by an eccentric old lady who made a living by selling orchids and pot plants, and charging admission to her zoo. She was a tough old bird with a wrinkled skin having weathered decades in the tropical sun. It was a very local affair containing a few wallabies, an olive python, small crocodiles and a number of parrots. Despite her rather gruff manner, typical of people known as 'Territorians True', she had a close understanding with her animals and birds and was also a local authority on Papua New Guinea flora. The language she used on her native employees made our hair stand on end, but the grins on their faces showed that they knew her bark was worse than her bite. One yell from her was enough to empty the 'Boihouse' of unwanted free loaders.

When she realised that we were interested in birds, she showed us a cage full of large, brightly coloured parrots, amongst which we noticed a small, rather drab in comparison, green fellow, looking a bit forlorn. He had belonged to someone who'd gone south and she'd been asked to give the bird a home. Our sympathy for the orphan was no doubt apparent in our faces and gave her the opportunity to offload the little chap. Before we knew it, we were relieved of ten dollars and were the owners of another bird. We named him Toby.

Toby came home and was introduced to Tatters. There was immediate jealousy between the two. Tatters, as the senior resident, ignored his very existence, and Toby made several friendly overtures but when they were rejected, he threw caution to the wind and began to tease her.

He developed a peculiar dance, consisting of a swaying movement and a sideways run with his beak along the floorboards towards the dignified Tatters, who looked down her nose at the approaching fool. On reaching his target, he would nip playfully at her feet and look up her slender legs like an old roué in a Parisian nightclub. Tatters, with head held high, would give a dainty sidestep, like an aristocrat avoiding something unpleasant.

We were not actively looking for animals or birds, far from it, but it almost seemed that they were looking for us, sensing by mysterious telepathic vibes that we couldn't ignore any creature in distress.

It was towards the end of a three p.m. to eleven p.m. shift at the receiving station at the other side of Jackson's airstrip when I unbolted the door and stepped outside for a breath of fresh night air. I exercised caution, holding a .22 Browning semi-automatic rifle while I scanned the dimly lit veranda for any sign of a Papuan black or taipan. I relied heavily on a natural instinct, developed during my childhood formative years in India: the sound of a tiny warning bell in my mind when a snake was in close proximity. After a pause, I walked out, feeling quite safe.

I always carried the rifle for self-assurance. The station was situated seven miles from town, completely isolated in a sea of savannah, comprising bush and kunai grass. There had been a couple of murders in the area recently, as yet unsolved, and on a lonely night watch, a fertile imagination could be nurtured by sounds from outside, or by the lack of them. Snakes were the biggest problem, particularly on the narrow airport perimeter road leading to the station. They were attracted to the light spilling out from the building, hunting green tree frogs which attached themselves to the plate glass windows with their spatulate, sucker-like feet. I sometimes rode a motorcycle to work and on numerous occasions had been unable to stop in time and had run over snakes, some of them long enough to span the road. My legs would reach for the sky as I felt the double bump, and I always had the feeling that the reptile had spun round and was now a pillion passenger.

One evening, a fellow worker was comfortably seated in the toilet when a tree frog flew through the louvred window behind him and attached itself to the far wall with a soft plop. He had barely lowered his newspaper when a ten-foot carpet snake slithered over the louvre glass panel and used his shoulder as a prop for onward progression, intent on pursuit. Utter confusion reigned for a while in the confined space and somehow all three managed to find an escape route.

I took a little walk outside on the gravel, wondering if I might see the mate of the Papuan black I'd killed earlier in the evening. During a lull in watch-keeping duties, I had decided to plant a custard apple seedling just outside the front window. I had dug a hole and looked around for suitable compost. At the base of the cyclone wire fence there was a pile of grass and other debris swept down by recent rain. It was well compacted and despite a cautionary nudge in my mind, I put the spade aside and used my hands to lift off a foot-high wad of compost and there, touching the knuckles of my right hand, was a shiny, wet Papuan black. My approach to the pile must have been soft and silent and he was obviously in a somnolent state because I had a half second advantage to use the spade.

I had taken the snake inside and examined it at my leisure, admiring the lethal fangs and cool, muscular body. I knew that the officer who would open the station the next morning was terrified of snakes, so with a perverse sense of humour, I had coiled the reptile up into a natural position and placed it in the refrigerator, head forward, poised to strike at any intruder. Thinking about it made me decide to go inside to check on the chilling effect and to possibly adjust the snake's position. Something hard, jagged, yet furry touched me on the shin. Tactile response was instantaneous. My scalp crawled and I leapt sideways.

A young black cat, just past the kitten stage, stood looking at me, with just one yellow eye, unperturbed by my sudden movement. The other eye was covered by a hard, jagged scab and this is what had touched me first. The little thing had obviously used up many of its nine lives. She must have been abused by humans and yet she showed pleasure at finding me. That she had survived so long out in the bush was amazing, but her diet of lizards and grasshoppers had only been just enough for her survival. I squatted down and spoke my thoughts out aloud. 'What are you doing here?' She came to me with a sideways gait, tail held high, and then arched her back and butted me with the blind side of her face.

I took her into the station and struck up a one-sided conversation while she lapped a saucer of milk. I then put her on the table and examined her thoroughly while she walked in tight little circles, purring up a storm. The wound was extensive, caused either by a hurled stone or an axe. She must have suffered agony during the first weeks, alone in the scrub, nursing her grievous wound, and, when hunger forced her, using her one good eye to hunt. My heart went out to her. She looked at me with a solemn yellow eye while I probed her ruined face with a gentle finger. The scab was as hard as rock and the surrounding area was leathery, through which a sparse growth of fur was growing. I called her Tramp and picked her up, holding her close to my chest, and swore to her that she was going to be all right.

I took her out to the Kila Kila animal clinic the next day and watched the gruesome business. Attempts to soften the scab for an examination of the eye behind it were futile. It was too thick and filled the entire socket. She was anaesthetised and the crushed, grape-like mass was scraped out, leaving the socket bare, and then the eyelids were sutured together.

She recovered rapidly from the operation and a week later the stitches were removed. Within a fortnight, with good food and care, she had put on weight, fur had grown over the left side of her face and she looked quite pretty. She soon learnt the rules of the house, mainly that Tatters and Toby were not to be touched. They accepted Tramp readily, and with some collusion looked upon her as another partner in mischief. Tramp was still kittenish enough to join in games and enjoyed giving Toby a cuff over the ear, propelling him along the floor like a shuttlecock. Tanya sized up the situation, noting that Tramp had a vulnerable blind side and during their games would attack from her blind quarter. However, generally speaking, Tramp was too restless to make a contented household cat and had her wandering periods, and no doubt due to her earlier experiences, she seized opportunities as they were presented, making off with the odd lamb chop.

She turned into a svelte young female and inevitably became pregnant, having delighted a battle-scarred Tom from across the street, adding her claw marks to his hide during their tryst, all of it to the accompaniment of hissing, spitting and long drawn out moans. The noise, coupled with the flapping of flying foxes and dull thuds as ripe mangoes fell on our tin roof, was not conducive to restful sleep.

At about this time, we heard from an acquaintance that a lady in the Konedobu area wanted to get rid of a half-Siamese kitten. Her thoroughbred sealpoint had committed an indiscretion, having a furtive affair with a low-grade tom. Due to a lack of muscle tone, the cat had been unable to bear her kittens naturally and was given a Caesarian section. Only one of the four survived. She was considering drowning it, something totally abhorrent to us, and we took it off her gladly.

We thought of a suitable exotic, oriental name and came up with Taiyuan, the name of a ship I had served on, on the China Coast. We now had five pets whose names all started with the letter T. I'd stutter sometimes trying to call or admonish them. Tanya the terrier, Tatters the bowerbird, Toby the parrot, Tramp the one-eyed cat and now Taiyuan the half-Siamese.

Taiyuan was introduced to the rest of the menagerie on the back veranda, and after being initially downtrodden and servile during her kittenish stages, she gradually reversed the situation and, using her inherent intelligence, turned things around. As the weeks and months went by, she exerted her influence and was not content until she had reached the top of the pecking order. At mealtimes, she expected, and got, her own dish, somewhat removed from the other ill-tempered members, and would stage a grand entrance. During the meal, she ate with decorum in contrast to the noisy snuffling from the other end of the veranda. She was amenable but aloof, pleasant yet condescending, to all except Annette, for whom she reserved a special devotion. She was beautiful, jet-black with a white blaze on her chest and two front paws, a long slender body with a shiny coat, and long black legs.

It was at this stage that I began to state loudly that we were to have no more animals or birds. Enough was enough!

One afternoon, I heard unfamiliar sounds coming from next door. The sound of water from a hose being sprayed into a box, coupled with faint mewings. On investigating, I found the boy next door, a young bully, happily hosing three kittens in the bottom of a tea chest. They were already almost submerged and a minute or two would have been too late. I gave him a clip on the ear and rescued them. They were no more than a few days old, blind and squirming in my hands, bedraggled, coughing and sneezing, pushing their little pink paws every which way. They were dried with a towel and fed warm milk soaked in cotton wool, and a squirt of Pentavite, of course. There was nothing wrong with their sucking powers because the wool was completely drained through three little teats which their sucking had created. They took up residence in a drawer of a spare cupboard on the veranda, with Tanya sniffing the air gap, cocking her ears to each mewing sound.

It wasn't long before they were drinking out of a saucer – at least the two black and white ones were – but there's always an odd one in most families. The third, a nondescript tabby, whom we named Thomas, the doubter, was convinced that the milk on the other side of the saucer was better. While his brothers were content to neatly lap it up from one side, Thomas would surf his way across and lie spread-eagled in the milk, lapping it up from the other side. When he was finished, the cleaning problem was solved by holding him up by the scruff of his neck and letting Tanya lick him dry, back, front and sides and under the tail. This is how a love affair was born between the two. We managed to find good homes for two of the kittens, but were left with Thomas, who was not admired by anyone else but us.

Qualim, our house-boi, had long ago accepted the idiosyncrasies of his Taubada and Sinabada. No doubt we were discussed in the neighbouring Rigo boi-houses, and the general opinion must have been favourable because he continued his excellent work and had made a friend of Tatters. 'Tathus' he called the bird, and was often seen standing in front of the cage opening his mouth in a wide smile, showing his betel-nut-stained teeth.

Toby, the parrot, proved to be less amenable to Qualim's overtures, taking an odd nip at his feet and delighting in pulling pegs off the line just minutes after Qualim had hung the laundry out. There was a stand-off between them. As a reward for his patience, I bought him an old floor polisher. This not only enhanced his status in the local boi-houses but assuaged his penchant for pulling apart electrical gadgetry. He accepted failure only after a great deal of experimentation, and when that happened, I'd find the polisher prominently displayed in the middle of the lounge, surrounded by nuts and bolts. The next day, Qualim would be on his hands and knees polishing the floor with a huge, wadded bunch of pawpaw leaves in the time-honoured method, but obviously he preferred mechanisation.

He'd keep remarking to Annette in sorrowful tones, 'Im buggerup', referring to the silent machine.

Later, we were to learn that a machine which was totally wrecked would be classed as 'Im buggerup tru'.

Qualim came to us within a day of our arrival. The neighbour's house-boi, with his ear to the ground, knew of our impending arrival and had made arrangements well in advance. House-bois of various tribal groups tend to occupy whole suburbs and streets within, and frown upon encroachment when one of their own 'won toks', or friends, are readily available. He may be a Rigo, a Kerema or a Mumeng. A few years ago, they were easily distinguishable, with variations in hairstyle and dress, but nowadays with the advent of urbanisation and the standard uniform of shorts, shirt and a European hairstyle, it's hard to tell. Qualim maintained his traditional style and individuality by keeping his Rigo hairstyle and had a bush on his head more than a foot high, and was bare-chested and wrapped a spotless laplap around his waist.

Payday was once a week and when he received his six dollars, I often wondered how he could survive on it, when it cost nearer to fifty for a European to live on for the same period. The wonder was that he managed to save some of it, to buy a transistor radio, have an occasional binge and have some left over for the Rigo privy purse to which he had to contribute regularly. Out of general mistrust for others, he'd hide his savings under the mattress of our spare bed. However, an increasing number were overcoming their suspicions and were getting savings books. Qualim hadn't reached that stage.

Qualim, Annette and I got on fine. The ideal situation is one where the Sinabada, Taubada and house-boi treat each other with mutual respect. He had a job to do and did it according to a set routine. Familiarity out of a sense of kindness tended to embarrass him. He was not a downtrodden, underfed servant with a beggar-like mentality looking for crumbs, but an individual in his own right who sought employment in a European household, and his responsibility wasn't a light one.

Understandably, Qualim and Tanya became allies, suffering harassment in common from the birds. We often wondered whose dog Tanya was, because more often than not she'd be in Qualim's boi house, sharing its simple comfort and his evening meal of brown rice mixed with mackerel pike from a tin. In fact, this is precisely what the cat's and Tanya's evening dinner consisted of. There were no butchers in Moresby. But their dinner was relished also by Tatters and Toby, who judiciously hung around on the periphery of Tanya's snapping range, darting in every now and then to snatch a delicious, lowly grain of rice. There was never much left but even so, whatever fragments remained were appreciated by the toads which emerged and surrounded the plate in a circle every evening, illuminated by a pool of yellow light from the veranda. A toad would seemingly stare into space, with infinite patience, unblinking, immobile, letting the gears mesh, and then make a small movement forward, and in that instant a grain of rice from the far rim would vanish. With similar economy of movement, others in the circle would dip forward in turn and like magic the plate would be clean.

Tanya accepted the situation, having learnt that chasing toads resulted in a frothy mouth. I found the toads fascinating and afforded them my protection and they too became part of the family. I could recognise male from female and, by picking up a male and stroking his back, could make him talk in a crazy kind of gurgle. I intrigued the toads by occasionally playing a long playing record of calls made by thirty-four species of frogs and toads of the USA and Canada. They were an attentive audience.

4

We bought a Peugeot 403 with a view to doing some exploring. Way back in the 1960s, the roads around the Moresby area were pretty restricted, with tar stretching only a few miles, followed by a rapid deterioration into gravelled tracks and finally bush roads. Apart from the climb to the Rouna Falls and Woodie's Hotel, there was a limited track down the Rigo Road and in the opposite direction the road to the Laloki River, further on to the Brown River, and further still, the Vanapa River.

The Rouna Falls Road was quite precipitous with steep climbs leading to the Sirinumu Dam and wooded hills, but the Rigo Road was bordering the coast and threaded its way through savannah country, fairly easily traversed. The Brown River Road went through dense jungle: jungle that closed in around you, matted and dense with trees climbing out of the undergrowth, reaching for the sky. The forest was three-tiered: the undergrowth, with its close-packed bush, harbouring reptiles; the middle layers allowing breathing space, dappled sunlight and the passage of breezes; and then the arboreal area, hundreds of feet high. It was a massive ecological system, hundreds of square miles in extent, virtually unspoilt and inhabited by millions of insects, snakes of all description – birds, including birds of paradise, wallabies, wild pigs, iguanas, cus cus, jungle fowl and goura pigeons. Swamps inside the forest had crocodiles, giant perch, tilapia, barramundi and eels.

One day, we set off and chose the Brown River Road. At that time, I was regrettably still at the stage where my hunting killing instincts had not been sublimated by the purer motives of conservation. It was hard to deny the habits of an entire adolescent period, gun in hand on the Indian plains, hunting, shooting and fishing. I was eager to try the

New Guinea jungle after years spent in the forests of the Himalayan foothills.

With Annette, Qualim, shotgun and ammunition, we set off, drove for an hour, and between the Laloki and Brown Rivers we turned down a forest road which sent a finger into the jungle and came to a dead end. While Annette and I were heavily shod, Qualim was barefooted, dependent on the hard leather of his soles for protection, and a T-shirt and lap lap completed his outfit. Though he was a Rigo boy and a savannah native, the jungle would be no stranger to him and his instincts, which I privately conceded were honed better than mine in this environment.

We locked the car and walked into the undergrowth, with me leading and scanning the immediate area ahead for reptiles. The undergrowth got thicker and began to drag at our knees and hips. There was the sound of wind through the branches hundreds of feet up, the swaying and rustling sounds of birds close by and distant, and up in the canopies the cooing of coura pigeons.

I tried to keep a mental picture of our progress and the back track we'd have to do to come back to our starting point. I was somewhat comforted by the knowledge that Qualim would have an unerring instinct of how to get out. It was oppressively hot and steamy though only ten o'clock in the morning. Looking up through the middle jungle with its tangled foliage, it was difficult to get an accurate fix of where the sun was, diffused as it was by dappled light in a massive mesh of green.

We heard the raucous cackle of a jungle fowl and Qualim pointed a finger. I could have sworn it came from another direction, deceived by its ventriloquism. We began to track the sound and the hunting instinct took over, stepping silently, holding one's breath, crouched low, with Annette hanging onto my trouser belt. The fowl was close, emitting cackle of alarm. I crouched even lower and got a brief glimpse of a fowl about the size of a bantam hen, head up and preparing for flight, about thirty feet away. I fired the right cylinder barrel using a number four and rushed forward.

There was no bird. It was unbelievable to have missed at that range. In that split second between the decision to pull the trigger and the millisecond sighting down the barrel, the bird had launched itself, escaping the close-grouped charge. I searched but found nothing. But where was Qualim? I conjectured he'd circled around to flush the fowl towards me. Annette and I looked at each other. Hot and sweaty, we were breathing hard. The thought entered my mind, not with a jolt but ever so gently, that we were alone. We called out to Qualim repeatedly but there was no response. I fired into the air repeatedly. Still no Qualim.

About fifteen minutes elapsed. We were perplexed and decided to backtrack, looking left and right, looking for signs of our earlier passage. We were in a vast sea of jungle, hopefully heading for the spur where the car was. The Brown River Road was possibly no more than a mile away, but was it to the right or left? Standing still, mouths open, ears straining, we could hear no sound of vehicles, only the sighing of the breezes through the trees around us. We continued calling for Qualim as we pushed forward and I continued firing a shot into the air every few minutes. The shot would reverberate, the jungle would fall silent, we'd shout and wait, listening, but only hearing our heavy breathing.

An hour later, I accepted the awful truth that we were really lost. I realised that the sounds of the shots I was firing were being absorbed by the blanket of heavy foliage, thick tree trunks and passage of wind, and being deflected in many directions. Qualim would be searching for the sound in various areas. It was midday and our thirst was increasing. A big mistake was that we hadn't brought water bottles.

A terrible sadness came over me as I looked at Annette, just twenty-one. We'd only been married a few months. What had I done? There was a sense of panic and options flooded my mind. Stay where we were or move? We talked it over and decided to move in another direction. I knew we could be moving in circles. I'd read that a New Zealander had been lost in this very jungle and had never been found. The opinion of experts had been that when weak and exhausted, the pigs would have got him. I remembered the advice to stay away from rivers, which would harbour crocs. I would have welcomed a river or a swamp to assuage our thirst.

We blundered on and as we moved, the jungle closed in behind us. We pushed forward ten feet, turned to look back and there was no hint of our passage. By three in the afternoon, we were in a state of despair, very thirsty and with tongues slightly swollen. Wordlessly, we held each other. We just couldn't stand still and simply had to push on. As we stumbled through the undergrowth, we disturbed several groups of wallabies, the small forest dorcopsis: they hurtled between us in fright, one passing between Annette's legs. Once, I heard the grunt of pigs. I can't imagine how many snakes and lizards had slithered away at our approach. A flight of cranes flew low over the canopy, honking as they went. It meant that a swamp was possibly just a few miles away.

Totally, utterly lost, exhausted, thirsty and in the depths of despair, our brains shrouded in a dark shadow of fear. Dense jungle surrounded us, with the Brown River on one side, the Laloki on the other, with a road joining the two. But where? The vast Waigani swamp was between us and the savannah, and then the coast.

Even at noon, down on the forest floor it was dim, and now, as it was five o'clock, it began to get dark. We came to halt beside a large tree and sank down at its base. We were in a lather of sweat, hands and arms scratched. We had both picked up several leeches and I plucked them off as Annette averted her eyes. They were plump with the blood they'd sucked. I took stock of our situation. I had about fifteen shotgun cartridges left, all number fours, enough for pigs at very close range, but I doubted they'd attempt anything until they sensed we were too weak to resist. We could survive the night, despite our thirst, but the long hours of darkness, the mosquitos and mental anguish would take their toll and the next day would find us a lot weaker. If it rained, we had a chance and I sent an earnest prayer up, dear God! I had matches and could light a fire which would give us some comfort. My heart bled for Annette. She had not complained once, no recrimination, no tears, not a whimper.

I began to prepare the area around the tree, clearing branches and sweeping away leaf mould, pulling at creepers and making a clean area, free of vegetation, mainly to keep leeches away. I paused for a moment and looked up and saw a glint in the distant gloom, a definite glint. I saw it again, a flicker, and my legs began to move and in an instant I was like a charging animal, pushing through the undergrowth, fighting to close the gap towards the glint. I gave a hoarse cry and I saw a movement and then the shape of a Papuan native. He stood stock-still, a look of alarm on his face, and was preparing to unlimber his shotgun, which he was carrying over his shoulder: it was butt-first with two wallabies hanging from the barrel behind him. It was the barest glint of the gun.

There was an immense feeling of relief filling my chest and I felt Annette behind me breathing hard as she stumbled to keep up in my mad chase. Thank God! I knew a few words of Motu. Road was Dara. I blurted out the word over and over, 'Dara. Dara?' pointing ahead. The man understood, nodding and pointing into the distance and indicating that we follow him. There was no emotion in his face, just an unblinking stare, taking in the picture of strangers in an emotional state of distress. He moved forward silently in bare feet, weaving his way through the undergrowth on what to him was a well defined path. Our saviour in torn khaki shorts, bare-chested, leading us to safety.

It was a good hour before the jungle ceased suddenly and there in the dark was the road. I gave him the only thing I had of value: all the ammunition and the bandolier I carried, about ten cartridges. We were rewarded by a smile, showing us his stained teeth, and he quietly went back into the forest.

We began to walk slowly down the road, terribly tired and with a raging thirst. We'd been going since ten in the morning and it was now late evening. The lights of a car a long way off gave us hope. It was a dead straight road and it took a long time to reach us. It was a utility with a white man in the driver's seat and a Papuan woman beside him. He rolled his window down and saw our dishevelled state and asked us what happened. I detected a Dutch accent. A Dutchman and his native wife, ready to take us to safety. I blurted out our story and he immediately took the top off a lemonade bottle.

'Be careful, man, sip slowly,' he said as he held it out to us.

We let the lovely liquid trickle slowly down our throats. The relief was heaven-sent. He opened another bottle. He owned a trade store near the Vanapa.

We clambered aboard in the back and he drove down the road towards the Brown River, looking for the spur we'd followed into the jungle. We came to it a few miles further on, turned down it and followed it into the jungle, and after half a mile there was the car, and beside it Qualim. When he saw us, he began to cry, unashamedly, tears running down his face. He grabbed our hands. It was too much and we began to bawl. Qualim spoke rapidly to the Papuan woman, who nodded repeatedly and then translated. Evidently, he had gone to the main road and stopped several cars telling the drivers that his Taubada and Sinabada were lost and to tell the police. As it later turned out, no one had done so.

We gave our heartfelt thanks to the Dutchman and his wife. I started the car and headed back to Moresby, to safety, to life, food, water and a bath.

We lay in the still of the night, silent, thinking, going back to our lucky escape. With the moonlight casting its segmented softness through the slatted louvres, aware of the waves lapping on Ela Beach, the flapping of flying fox wings outside and the gentle whirr of the overhead fan. I'm fairly certain that our son, Richard, was conceived that night.

5

Twelve months to the day after our arrival in Port Moresby, our son was born. However, before this coming event, both Annette and I had expressed a view that I should be present at the birth. The matron of the female unit at the hospital flatly refused: it just wasn't done. Annette was furious. Also, my workmates had similar views to the matron, saying I should be at the Moresby Hotel in Musgrave Street, celebrating with a few beers while my wife did all the work.

We made a sustained attack on the attitude of the matron, and the hospital, enlisting the aid of our GP, who was sympathetic. We finally prevailed. We were creating a precedent in this part of the world. We felt that we were a team and it was a natural thing to do, and I had every right to be there, having sown the seed, as it were.

In order to induce the birth, we adopted the local and time-honoured method of going to see a movie at the drive-in at Ward Strip, which required a mile or so of driving on a corrugated, bumpy track, enough to shake things up a bit. It worked.

It started, as most births do, in the early hours of the morning. We were well prepared, having read Grantley Dick-Read's book on natural childbirth from cover to cover. In fact, it was one of the first things I picked up when the time came. The book had prepared us for the facts of childbirth but not the associated emotional experience.

We checked into Taurama Hospital at about three a.m. and were shown into a spartan room, having just a single bed and pillow, and a chair. Emerging from the walls was an array of pipes and valves. The European nurse and her Papuan trainee made infrequent visits. I did the counting and timing between contractions, giving little bits of advice and wondering when the GP would arrive. The pain was increasing and with no one attending, I began to experiment with the mask and valves on the wall. I put the mask on my face and inhaled and heard no hissing. I fiddled a bit more, took some deep breaths and nearly fell off the chair in a daze, thankfully short-lived.

The GP arrived and an hour of noise ensued, with sounds of straining and pushing, heavy breathing and moaning, with commands to do this or that, but Annette was only listening to my voice and the doctor relayed his commands through me.

There was sheer physical effort and then a miracle happened. I saw the first glimpse of a head emerging and told Annette that the hair was dark, then a bit more, the crumpled face, shoulders, giving her a commentary, and then he slid out and I was able to tell her he was a boy. Annette lay back totally exhausted, listening to her son lose his cool, as angry as a hornet with tiny fists clenched as a tube was pushed down his throat to remove mucus, and then the ultimate moment of joy when the little wrapped bundle was placed in her arms.

It was much later, years in fact, before I had the courage to express what I'd seen: a slippery, slimy, reddish-purple, toothless and wrinkled bundle, about a hundred years old.

In truth, within an hour, he had smoothed out, a handsome little fellow, warm and blissfully asleep, totally unaware of the world he'd entered.

Following this happy event, we had a tragedy. Tramp, the one-eyed orphan, was killed while Annette was still in hospital, but I kept the news to myself. There was an inherent inevitability of it happening, with her one-eyed restricted visibility putting her at a disadvantage. Our house was built into the bottom of a steep hill with common steps leading to the house above ours. A couple, accompanied by their Alsatian dog, frequently visited the neighbours above us. On one occasion, we met these people on the steps while Annette was carrying Taiyuan, the half Siamese. The cat, seeing the dog, jumped from her arms and the woman immediately urged the dog to give chase. We were temporarily speechless. Annette made frantic efforts to stop the animal, but fortunately, Taiyuan was fast enough to find a tree. A furious exchange of words followed, and the woman, as bold as brass, said she'd taught the dog to chase cats because she didn't like them. Her husband muttered what appeared to be an apology.

These people were of a type found all too frequently in the Islands. Australian nomads, in their mid-thirties, drifting along the Northern Territories, Dutch New Guinea, Papua New Guinea and Solomon Islands belt. Their dog was kept to deter what they referred to as kanakas. One of their acquaintances, a man living on Three Mile Hill, trained dogs, generally Alsatians, for this specific purpose by the simple method of putting a young dog in a sack, giving it a sound thrashing and then forcing his house-boi to release the animal. The dog saw a dark native face and all its pain and anger was henceforth channelled in a tunnel of hate towards the perpetrator.

While Annette was in hospital, I had been keeping a close eye on one-eyed Tramp, as she was expecting her first litter. I came home to find her dead on the doorsteps. She had been badly mauled and mutilated. I felt the loss keenly. She'd had a hard time before I found her, but since then, with love and care from us, she'd grown into a beautiful animal. Qualim and I buried her and I placed a small cross at the head of her grave.

Qualim told me he'd seen the Alsatian around earlier, and urged revenge. 'Shoot im, Taubada!' he said, extending an index finger and curling it around an imaginary trigger.

A charge of rat shot had crossed my mind, but I couldn't explain to him that the dog had been badly trained, and it wasn't the dog that needed shooting.

I gave Annette the bad news, which only made her more determined to leave the hospital. The baby, Richard James, had thrush, mosquitos were plaguing the ward, and there was a smell drifting over from the native section where the patients had blocked the sewerage system by using coconut husks to wipe themselves instead of toilet paper.

A few friends came over to help us celebrate Annette's return and of course to see the young son and heir. We sat in the lounge room, joined as usual by our animals and birds. Tanya was smiling all over, wagging her tail and sticking close to Annette. Taiyuan sniffed at the baby, blinked her eyes a few times and then removed herself, like a snubbed prima donna, no longer in the limelight. Tatters hopped around pecking at shoelaces. Toby the parrot and Thomas started their new game. Toby would walk around the edge of the round cane basket and Thomas would give him a left or right hook, sending him to the bottom. However, this time, Toby had picked up on his new indulgence of having a sip of rum and Coke from sundry glasses set on the floor beside the chairs and was rolling around like a drunken sailor, leaving Thomas quite perplexed. He kept falling into the basket on his own accord.

At about this time, we received an unexpected present. A coastal skipper with steamships, Gordon Keeble, on the gulf run to Baimuru presented us with a blue-tongued lizard, about two feet long, as thick as my forearm and in prime condition. According to Gordon, it was a humanitarian gesture. While at anchor off a village, a number of native craft approached carrying produce, one with a platform on which a score of lizards were displayed, and the owner was methodically breaking their backs, which was, in the absence of refrigeration, the traditional way of keeping them alive but immobile, and the meat fresh. Gordon bartered quickly and bought this one while it was still unharmed.

We named her Tallulah, after the actress Tallulah Bankhead. I promptly converted a packing case into a cage, filling it with debris of suitable rocks, leaf mould and such home comforts. Tallulah had to be force-fed at first, with juicy bits of raw liver and meat. Blue-tongues may appear sluggish but can move like lightning and I had to move twice as fast. I'd feint with one hand in front and grab her by the neck with the other and then hang on as she twisted her tail around my forearm to get a purchase, trying to break my grip. At some stage during this wrestling, I'd shove a piece of meat down her gullet. In due course, she began to feed herself and afforded me enough recognition to desist from making a lunge when I placed meat in her cage. Nobody else could go near her – not that anyone wanted to. With Tallulah in her cage, brooding malevolently, the birds were safe and still free to use the back veranda, and the lizard was relatively safe from Qualim, who had once mentioned that she was 'Planti good kai kai'. She was fat enough and at Koki Market would have fetched a good price.

Tanya in particular was very cautious, perhaps because of a previous incident involving something that looked like Tallulah, only much larger. We were visiting a friend, the chief fisheries research officer at Kanudi Research Station, and Tanya had come along for the ride. It was a very interesting place with a mass of laboratory equipment, jars containing fish, and sea snakes, turtles in tanks, and large zinc-lined boxes containing small sharks. There were crocodile heads preserved in formalin, and outside several cages holding live crocodiles. Their growth rate was being studied.

Tanya, with her tail erect, wagging and following curious scents, came across a seven-foot crocodile lying immobile, hard up against the cyclone wire fence. She sniffed the creature cautiously through the wire, moving along its length starting from the tail end. I've never seen anything move so fast in all my life. When Tanya reached its head, the crocodile allowed her a cursory sniff, perfectly still, eyes shut, feigning sleep and then in the blink of an eyelid exploded into action, jaws agape and teeth slashing against the wire with a loud hiss, bowling Tanya off her feet in fright.

Crocodiles are particularly fearsome. There's no escape when seized by one. They produce nightmares. My father was nearly taken by one, and I was once in the unenviable position of being up to my chest in the Wakgani Swamp, hampered by weeds and within a few feet of retrieving a duck only to feel a powerful surge and have it plucked under as I was about to grasp it. I felt vulnerable to invisible jaws from my armpits down.

Gordon Keeble, who'd given us Tallulah, witnessed a horrible sight when steaming up the Fly River. On either side, there were wide mudflats stretching from the river to low, bush and tree-lined hills where a small village was located. A native searching for shellfish was knee-deep in the slush about thirty metres from the river bank and unknown to him a large crocodile was slithering towards him fast, and using the slimy mud to propel itself. The passengers on board began yelling and screaming, and Gordon blew the ship's whistle in almost continuous bursts but to no avail. The man turned, was transfixed, frozen in terror as the crocodile with jaws agape rushed at him and took him by the waist, rolled him over and over and then slithered back to the river. It was all over in less than half a minute.

Just a few weeks ago, I'd bought one for Annette, for a dollar, from a young Papuan girl. A little crocodile, about a foot long, full of fight. An accepted custom in Port Moresby was for young Papuan boys and girls to visit various offices, selling mangoes, shells, beads and occasional baby crocodiles. When this baby was pulled out of his basket, he came out hissing, wriggly madly, with jaws agape. He had a beautiful set of needle sharp teeth, and in case anyone forgot to look, he made sure by keeping his jaws open all the time. On second thoughts, I decided it would not get on with Tanya, the cats and birds. I gave it back to the girl and let her keep the dollar.

Most Papuan and New Guinea natives have an inherent fear of reptiles of any kind. In their villages, snakes and crocodiles form the natural hazards of life. One of the staff working in an adjoining office, a New Zealander, was a practical joker and kept pet snakes. Some time ago, he'd caused havoc in our office by releasing one of his large olive pythons. A Papuan clerk had given the alarm when out of the corner of his eye he'd caught the movement of a snake making for a corner. He shrieked and leapt for higher ground on top of a desk. Within seconds, there was no one left at floor level, everyone making long Olympic-style leaps to safety. While chaos ensued, two of us with earphones on, sat at our desks continuing our concentration while receiving streams of high-speed morse signals, without a break.

I can vouch for the feats that people are capable of when in fright. During my childhood in India, we employed a punkah coolie, all of seventy years of age, whose job it was to pull the ropes to move the punkahs in our bedrooms, providing a semblance of cool air. When the punkahs stopped moving one night, my father awoke in a sweat and went onto the veranda to investigate. He saw a large cobra, erect and with his hood flared, facing the old coolie. It slithered away at my dad's approach. Behind the old man there was a metre-high, tiered flower pot stand. Amazingly, from a seated cross-legged position, Dad saw the old fellow do a backflip, over the stand and land on his feet.

Eventually, we decided it was time we moved to a larger and newer house. Apart from the canine, feline and avian influences, we now had the possibility of a crawling baby, and Annette was pregnant again. My application for a new house in the suburb of Boroko was approved. It was up on stilts, with a large area under it that was dry and protected, and the whole half-acre lot was enclosed by a cyclone wire fence. It was ideal for animals.

We tried to make the move as easy as possible for the animals. On moving day,, our own effects went over first, and I stayed in the new house with the baby while Annette and Qualim went back for the animals. They placed the birds in their cages on the back seat, Tanya sat on the shelf in the rear window, Thomas sat on top of Toby's cage and Taiyuan calmly sat on Tatters cage. Tallulah was placed on the front seat. Qualim squeezed himself in beside the birds. At the last moment, Annette heard the phone ringing inside the house and hurried in to answer it. When she came out, she found the car surrounded by tourists from a French tourist vessel which had berthed at the wharf. They thought they'd found another tourist attraction and were happily photographing and exclaiming over their find. The animals couldn't care less and it was only Qualim who sat there preening himself, smiling broadly and exposing his red betel-nut-stained teeth. Somewhat embarrassed, Annette squeezed her tummy under the steering wheel and drove off.

We kept the animals inside the house for a few days and then released them, except for Tallulah. All accepted the new environment, except neurotic Thomas, or Thomasina, who behaved as though her whole world had turned upside down. She acted as if pursued by shadows. On being released, she made a beeline for the gate with her belly low to the ground, crossed the road and disappeared into a monsoon drain. We were not unduly concerned and had expected some odd behaviour from her and anticipated that she'd make her way back towards dusk and dinner time. She remained in her refuge for a week, prey to her nameless terrors. We put food out for her which she ate under cover of darkness. We occasionally saw a round head and pointed ears over the lip of the drain. On the tenth day, she finally found the courage to come home, again with her belly scraping the ground, hugging all available cover, indentations in the road and tussocks of grass; putting on a final spurt to safety she flew up the steps into the house. Tanya immediately pounced on her, pinning her to the floorboards, and Toby waddled over to say hello. Thomas lay there unresisting, quietly accepting the paws that pinned her, happy to be home.

Thomas, Tanya and Toby and Tatters formed an affectionate foursome, later suffering a setback when Toby was found dead. He must have had a heart attack or something during the night. We were all upset, and pundits say that animals don't feel the way we do but we saw a change in Thomas, definitely more remote and looking sadder.

For a while, Qualim had seemed restless and we weren't surprised when he asked for permission to return to his village for a visit. He had already arranged a won tok to take his place. To our surprise and delight, when he returned a month later, he had a gift or us. It was a young, brightly coloured parrot. Her head and breast were scarlet, her back and wings were red, tinged with royal blue and when she spread her wings they were tipped with green. We were particularly impressed with the cage Qualim had brought her in. It was a sheet of bark, sewn together with natural fibres into a cylindrical shape; the bottom of the cage consisted of thin sticks pushed through holes in the bark, firmly fixed, but those at the top were readily removable to allow feeding and easy access to the bird. It was a simple, practical and artistic piece of work. It wasn't until months later when she got more plumage that we discovered what a rare and valuable bird we had. Sshe was a red-winged eclectus. We named her Tosca.

We gave her the run of the house, the stairway, the shrubs and the trees outside, after clipping her wings. She blossomed, and the scarlets and greens of her plumage were vivid. She was unique, being the female of the species that was brilliantly covered rather than the male, contrary to Nature's normal dictates. She loved being talked to, particularly when words of praise were uttered while gently lifting her wings and admiring the colours underneath. This became such a ritual that she would voluntarily raise her wings in anticipation.

6

I had an old Papuan friend, born and bred in Hanuabada, a coastal village adjoining the administration centre off Konedobu. He was a gentleman, a member of the flock of Rev. Percy Chatterton of the London Missionary Society.

Mea was addicted to betel-nut chewing, a quiet, polite man. He was the chief clerk in the communications office where I worked. He was the master of the accounts ledger, with beautiful calligraphy. It was irksome to see a man of his calibre, an elder of the Hanuabadans, aristocrats of the coastal people, being treated with contempt by Australians. The manager of the office was one in particular who, to put it bluntly, was of poor character and overly fond of beer. He could be seen on most afternoons under the mango trees outside the office, slumped in his car, mouth agape, sleeping off a liquid lunch.

Mea said little but he nurtured a deep hurt that our employer, a big communications corporation, appeared unwilling to give recognition to his loyalty. When the Japanese were pushing towards Kokoda, hammering on the back door of Moresby, Mea stayed behind and looked after the office and other company interests while others fled into the bush. Most employees of the South Pacific post who stayed behind were given proper recognition and rewarded with a handsome bonus. Some of the old hands of the post were friends of his. Mea's letters were eloquent in the extreme, one particularly, with the assistance of Percy Chatterton, was a masterpiece, but to no avail. It was an injustice and he bore it stoically, and in the manner of the time maintained a subservient mein. However, nothing could detract from his proud bearing. Still, to the local manager, Mea was a lazy, betel-nut-chewing kanaka.

Mea had a friend, an old craftsman who turned out excellent replicas of native lakatois: single-hulled canoes, or double-hulled, with an outrigger, a mast and bark sails in the traditional crab claw shape. They came in sizes from twenty centimetres to a metre in length, beautifully carved and subtly covered with bush pigments. I was interested in buying several and Mea agreed to introduce me to the old man, who it appeared was deliberately remote from the mainstream of life, content in traditional ways, reflecting on the past and viewing with disappointment and distrust the erosion of the old Papuan way of life. Elders like him could see their children becoming urbanised, forsaking old ways and forgetting a long heritage of culture, with its interwoven stories of myth and fact, songs and dances. The young were now in full pursuit of material things, the guitar and transistor radio, and looking for status. It was a lot different from the time, just passed, when social standing was based on the amount of body tattoos, hoardings of cowrie shells, sacks of flour and the number of pigs.

Some of the elders, along with interested Europeans, one of whom was Annette, who were aware of the dangers and were making serious attempts to keep the old culture alive by arranging sing-songs, festivals and eisteddfods and introducing new mediums. It was in the latter that Annette was mainly interested. She was giving piano lessons to Australian and Papuan students. She established an examination centre for the Australian Musical Education Board in Port Moresby.

I often recalled back in the 1950s, the sight of slender, tattooed, grass-skirted and bare-bosomed maidens were a normal part of the local scene. I was on the *Soochow*, a coastal freighter that ran up from Australia, visiting Moresby, Samarai, Lae, Madang, Rabaul and Kavieng. One was tempted to reach out and touch, but dare not. Besides, it would have been a sort of betrayal of trust, because they were unaware of the effect a naked upper torso could have on young Europeans. Still, their presence lent an interest to a fairly drab Musgrave street, leading towards Ela Beach.

There was an innocence about it, and acceptance of the status quo. Europeans, the colonial masters, could be forgiven their appreciation and general lapse into believing that they were living in an unspoiled frontier society that would be perpetuated forever. It was hard to believe that in the 50s I could casually walk off the ship, trailing a .22 rifle, walk up Musgrave Street, down to Ela Beach, and fire off numerous rounds out to sea, aiming at various bits of debris. No one seemed to notice.

All that was past. The girls were now neatly dressed in blouse and skirt, typists and stenographers or working behind the counters of Burns Philp or Steamships stores. The only bosoms exposed now were either huge and bulbous, or of the razor strop variety flaunted by some matrons whenever a tourist ship came in. They were enterprising ladies, mouths red with betel-nut juice, gyrating their grass-skirted hips and ululating in shrill tones. They smiled enticingly and held their hands out.

I went in search of old Mea. I had one of my hare-brained ideas of possibly exporting the miniature lakatois made by Mea's friend. I found Mea in his house, built on stilts out over the sea, one of several hundred, all more or less of the same plan: a large wooden-framed living area, partitioned by reed mats to make the requisite number of rooms, thatched roofs and a slatted wooden catwalk allowing contact with the shore and connected to a veritable maze of other catwalks linking the entire village. Chickens and pigs had their own compartments, attached to the house. All debris, everything, went into the sea below and was flushed away by the tide. Ashore, the palm trees waved lazily in the coastal breeze, with the earth at their bases packed hard to the consistency of concrete by the pressure of feet going to and from over the centuries. There was not a blade of grass or shrubbery to be seen and no area in which creepy crawling things could hide.

Mea led me to the old man's hut. He sat cross-legged, smoking a pipe, packed with a cut of imported Rhodesian tobacco – so much for the trade embargo with Rhodesia at the time! The halo of smoke around him blended with the smoke from a wood fire in a cutaway forty-four-gallon drum. Like the old man in front of me, everything was brown and smoke-stained. Mea acted as interpreter. I bought six of the lakatois at a set price per article, but when I suggested that if I bought fifty or sixty items there might be a reduction, the old fellow was apathetic to the idea. One or a hundred, it made no difference. In any case, he only intended making limited numbers, enough to enable him to buy his tobacco, betel nut and perhaps bush meat.

At the back of the room in the gloom, there was a large crate and I was aware of a thumping, scratching noise coming from it. The thump, when it came, was quick and sharp. I suspected there was a wallaby in there, as thumping their feet was one of their characteristics, of fear or warning. I could picture the terrified animal in there, in the darkness, destined no doubt to be butchered. My fertile imagination saw the singeing of its hair, skewered and roasted over a lazy, smoking fire. It had probably been trapped days ago, stuffed into a gunny sack and then dumped into the crate. My mind ran riot. I knew that the tiny dorcopsis forest wallabies that one could see laid out in rows in Koke Market cost a few dollars. They were the size of a rabbit, small enough to be bowled over by a shotgun blast, but this one was bigger, probably an adult. I offered ten, the old man wanted fifteen but settled for twelve. The lid was inched back and a ferocious struggle ensued with the wallaby, in terror, in full flight within the confines of a two-metre crate, ricocheting off the sides, thumping its hind legs in total alarm. The old man finally grabbed it by the neck and drew it out. It was like spring steel, all muscle gyrating under the two-handed grip around its neck. We put it in a sack and carried the struggling prisoner to the car.

On the way back, we again passed through Konedobu, the administrative centre for the entire country. It was an enclave with some substantial, white-painted brick buildings, with lawns and clumps of bougainvillea, shaded by palm trees and scores of lookalike clapboard offices, raised up on stilts. This was where the bulk of expatriate whites worked, grooming a vast indigenous clerical staff for the eventual takeover. The Civil Service was well in place, with a smooth transition being the aim, when the time came.

I couldn't help recalling the last time I'd visited this place. It was way back in the 50s, when the *Soochow* first came into Papuan waters on a more or less scouting, probing visit. The shipping company I worked for, with headquarters in Hong Kong, was losing its mainland China routes, following the Communist takeover, and had decided to send a couple of ships to the Australia-New Guinea area, to take on Burns Philp and judge the response from shippers and agents. The second mate and I were imbued with the romance of it all, spurred on by the sight of coral reefs, white sandy beaches and dense coconut plantations.

On one of our visits to Moresby, we asked for and were granted an interview with the deputy director of agriculture. We were ushered into a large room cooled by a revolving roof fan. Rattan blinds kept the sun out. We stated our hopes of becoming plantation owners. In response to his query, we said that we had a thousand pounds sterling between us. The gentleman took that in and allowed a hint of a smile to soften his face while he gave thought to our proposal. He asked if we knew anything about coconuts. No, but we were prepared to learn. He sat back and reflected for a few moments and shook his head slowly. He gave us full marks for trying, adding that such a venture required considerable experience and much more capital; besides, we would never be able to compete with the native owners, nor the Chinese, who were heavily involved in the New Britain and New Ireland areas. His advice was much the same as was given to us when we approached the commissioner in Brunei, Borneo, when we asked for his views on the possibility of our starting a chicken farm. He also gave us a sad smile and shake of his head.

We named the wallaby Terence. With Qualim's help, I put him in a strengthened chicken run, sheltered by several banana clumps, and within a week he settled in well, not attempting to flee and accepting fodder and chopped-up kau kau, sweet potato. A month later, again with Qualim's help, I put a dog collar on him, with a short chain, and through the ring in the collar I ran a rope from a shady tree in the middle of the front lawn, through some shrubbery, and tied the other end to an upright under the house. He was quite happy hopping around and on occasion could be seen lying on his side contentedly in the sun. Tanya was told that Terence was a member of the family, and *no*, he was not to be chased.

It was all working well. Terence had shelter, green grass to crop, supplemented by bananas and kau kau. Months passed and I moved him from time to time. Then we had an incident that broke our hearts. We went to the drive-in one night and came home to find him hanging from a low branch, his hind legs barely inches from the ground. I moved very fast, gathered up his body in my arms, rocking him like a baby. Annette was in tears. He was still warm and I gave him mouth to mouth resuscitation, saying to him, over and over. 'Breathe, Terence, breathe!!' His glazed eyes grew dull and sadly I had to give up. I blamed myself for not taking the chance of releasing him earlier, just to hop around at will freely. It was a sad night and we both shed tears. On the following day, I took him to the other side of Jackson's airstrip, to an area of wartime bunkers and disused taxiways and buried him under a cairn of rocks. It was typical wallaby country, with tall grass and coastal scrub. Sad, very sad!

Annette was given our next waif by a very contrite and almost tearful workmate of mine. She was giving a piano lesson to a Papuan girl when she heard a knock and went to the door and found Hooper with a little joey wrapped in a handkerchief. He stammered that it was all an accident and he was so sorry. He didn't know what to do except come to us. Through the windows of the receiving station, he'd seen a mob of wallabies moving through the grass, grazing. He'd recently bought a pistol and he took a test shot at what he said was extreme range. Unfortunately, it was a fluke head shot. After finishing his shift, he went out into the tall grass and found the dead wallaby, and in the pouch was this little joey. He drew it out, put it in his handkerchief and came to the only people he knew who would know what to do. Annette let him in and could see how crestfallen he was as he told her how it had happened. She took the pink little thing from him, totally without fur. It was really lucky to be alive.

Attempts to make it suck voluntarily on a cotton ball soaked in diluted Carnation milk were unsuccessful, but fortunately we had a doll's bottle, which worked marvellously. We put him in a shoebox, snug and warm in old nappies, and were happy to see him survive the first night, holding his own through the next day, and he slowly showed signs of ongoing survival with a little nicely rounded pink belly. Annette was now fully confident of success and ran up a pouch on our new Elna sewing machine. We named him Timothy. He weighed eight ounces.

Timothy grew up fast and regarded Annette as his mother and was never further than a foot from her, bounding on his hind legs, behind her, down the hallway from the bedroom to the kitchen, to the lounge, back and forth. Like all young creatures, he was full of the joy of living, and much like a lamb, a pup or a kitten, he'd make vertical leaps, land with a twist and accelerate down the hallway at great speed, slip on the polished floor and ricochet off the walls, erupt into the lounge, do a zig and a zag and slip-slide his way towards the door where his pouch was hanging. He became very adept at taking flying leaps and scoring a bullseye as he entered his pouch.

In order to feed him regularly, Annette took him shopping in his pouch in the main Steamship or Burns Philp stores and he behaved perfectly, despite being stared and giggled at. Local Papuans tolerated the idiosyncrasies of the Europeans, but privately I'm sure they evaluated how much meat there would be on this little Magani.

At the drive-in theatre , Timothy was quite content to hang on the door handle, and during intervals he'd hop around and do his business. Sometimes he had diarrhoea, and then it was essential to have plastic liners fitted to his pouch, and he had to have his bottom wiped.

As he grew up, he got the urge to wander: grass was always greener on the other side of the street, and the neighbouring boi-house garden had better sweet potatoes than ours. Word was passed down the road that Timothy was not to be harmed, a wish that was respected. He'd go walkabout quite often and it was quite amusing to see him being brought back. When he was small, it was a simple matter of picking him up, but when he became a young adult, he would resist. A couple of bois would have a paw each, pulling him along while he applied the brakes, digging his heels in. The bois giggled, admonishing him, 'Timoti, yu pella no good magani.'

Sometimes, he'd break free and sit back on his tail, head up and front arms raised in a boxing stance. The bois would let out a whoop and dance in front of him, urging him on. I'm afraid I used to encourage his boxing tactics, particularly as he grew older. We'd have a ding-dong battle, jabbing left and rights, sparring with each other, and at times it became quite hectic. While trying to get inside my guard, his long claws would rake my forearms, causing long red weals from elbow to wrist, some bleeding and quite deep. Annette and the lady next door would be horrified, sure that I would get tetanus, and they would go pale at my homemade cure: a bowl of hot water into which almost a cup of salt would be stirred, and using a large wad of cottonwool soaked in the solution I'd grit my teeth and scour my forearms, dry them and apply antiseptic cream.

Even though I'd connect a few times, he never bore ill will and no matter how fierce our engagement, at a certain point I'd duck in, grab and lift him up bodily so that his front was upward and his face was tucked in against my neck, and he would proceed to lick my throat, all belligerence forgotten. As he grew bigger, picking him up became quite a strain, and our games became less frequent.

Life went on happily. Entertainment and dining out was limited to just a couple of restaurants providing European cuisine, the Moresby Hotel, or a Chinese restaurant in Boroko: there was the Papuan movie theatre, which was definitely full of fleas, and the drive-in at Ward's Strip. The latter was very popular despite having to wait for quite lengthy periods while all the cars moved off, headlights piercing the huge clouds of dust.

It was in reduced visibility with swirling dust when coming home one night when I saw a small brown pup, transfixed in the glare of the headlights and at the very last moment it scurried into the bush beside the road. An immediate mission of mercy drew me out of the car and, stepping carefully, very aware of snakes, I searched the verge, pushing shrubbery aside and found it trembling against the trunk of a small tree. It made a feeble growl and snapped at my hand as I picked it up. It had a large wound on top of its head. For just a second, I wondered what I was doing, but in the next moment it was inconceivable that I could abandon it. We took her home and set about cleaning her up. With Dettol and cotton wool, we bathed the wound and exposed a jagged hole, which we dusted with antiseptic powder. The little thing lapped readily at the warm milk, but the milk immediately reappeared, running out of her nostrils. It was very late, so we put her and ourselves to bed.

The next day, I took her to the vet at Kila Kila, and he diagnosed the problem. The wound, he conjectured, was caused by a blow from a stone, but the pup probably had a bone or something in her mouth and the blow had caused the object to pierce the roof of the mouth, hence the milk being sucked up and coming back through the nasal passages. He anaethetised the poor creature and did what he could to close the hole with suturing. He was confident that the hole would close over.

We called her Tramp, in honour of the earlier Tramp. She was a mongrel, but the most faithful dog we ever owned. Single-minded devotion to Annette was her aim in life, and she was never more than a pace away. She had obviously been mistreated by natives and her bristling demeanour when one came too near was enough to promote a wide detour. It was a handy trait because at the time there had been a spate of rapes and attempted rapes, and the urbanisation of Moresby, the influx of people from outlying areas, and resulting unemployment gave indications that this kind of thing was on the increase. Annette had to be cautious when walking on Ela Beach, catching the evening breeze.

There had been an occasion much earlier – in fact, when she was pregnant – when down on Ela Beach a couple of young natives had come close. One grabbed her and started to fondle and tried to kiss her.

She fought back and bit the fellow on the lower lip, drawing blood, and they ran away. The matter was reported to the police and subsequently the culprits were caught, the split, swollen bottom lip identifying the perpetrator. They were taken behind the police station and subjected to an interrogation and confessed. After due process of the law, they were sent to Bomana prison to spend some time there.

Annette was giving music lessons to the twin daughters of the police inspector who handled the Ela Beach incident. He gave Annette a .22 rifle for safety. He told us the story of the gun. There was an old couple, 'Territorians True', who had a chicken farm on an island in Bootless Bay and employed a large number of natives. They were doing well supplying eggs and meat birds to Moresby. The old man died and his wife was now alone. She was expecting the episode that followed. The headman of the workers broke down the door to her bedroom and approached her. She was sitting up in bed with a loaded rifle and she gave him five rounds in the chest from the semi-automatic. She immediately phoned the police, gave her story and was put into protective custody and on the very next day was flown down to Cairns in order to avoid payback killing, which is a strong part of native culture.

I taught Annette the rudiments of handling a weapon, loading, ejecting, taking aim and the gentle squeeze of the trigger. We set up targets and she learned fast, becoming quite proficient. The fact that the lady of the house, the Sinabada, had a gun and capable of using it was well known in the area.

Annette and Richard travelled to Port Moresby on the historic *Bulolo*.

Upon arriving in Port Moresby, Annette and Richard found they had a house-boi already organised for them. Qualim became a great friend.

Annette and Richard visited the annual Mt Hagen Show, where all the tribes from New Guinea collected. They danced, had meetings, entered competitions, and sang.

Richard with Tatters, the bowerbird.

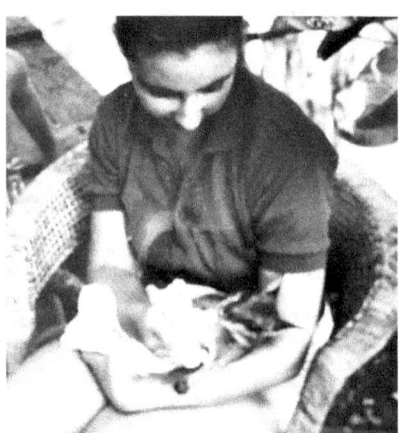

Annette feeding Timothy the baby agile wallaby with a toy baby bottle.

Toby (parrot) was the boss, and fed before the cats, who had to wait patiently.

Timothy lived with us for many years, until we thought he needed to mate. He went to Warrels Park Zoo. He invaded their kitchen and spread cooked porridge everywhere.

Tammy's wing was clipped by a bullet, and she was added to the menagerie.

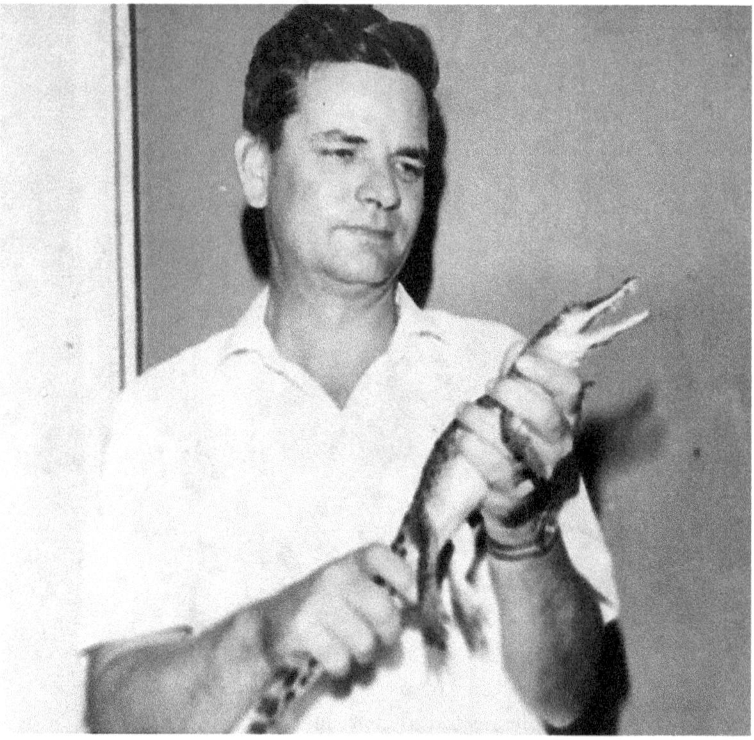

Rejected pet. Richard intended to add it to the animal family, but Annette was not keen. He escaped in the OTC office, and was never seen again.

Dorcopsis Forrest wallabies saved from the pot.

Encouraging the tiny ones to eat.

Richard with Timothy.

Our pets were taught to get on. Twitters the tame mynah bird was safe from Taiyan the Siamese cat.

Annette was Timothy the wallaby's mother,
and he was with her constantly.

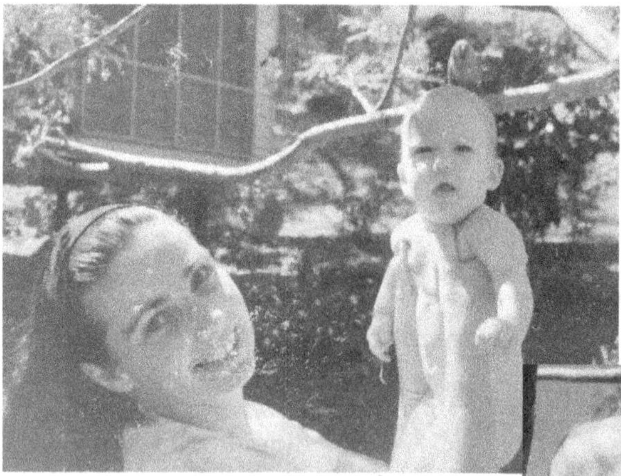

Annette and baby Kylie.
Tosca (rare red-winged ecclectus female parrot)
followed us everywhere, even in the garden.

Tosca watching baby Kylie
in the garden.

Annette, little Karen and baby Timothy the wallaby in the garden.

Richard with Twitters, our fawn=breasted bowerbird, Tramp and Tanya.

Annette in the garden with Tramp and Timothy.

Feety (rare albino Phalanger Maculatus Maculatus – a type of cus cus) watching us. She was very tame.

Feety reaching out for food.

Twitters (fawn-breasted bowerbird) was one of our first pets, and ruled the roost. She followed Annette everywhere.

Out on a day's exploring, with Tammy, Dick's dog, and Tramp, Annette's dog.

Above, right and left:
Dorcopsis wallabies that went to
Crandon Park Zoo, Miami, Florida.

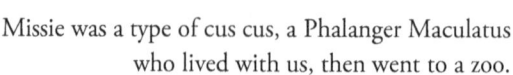

Missie was a type of cus cus, a Phalanger Maculatus
who lived with us, then went to a zoo.

We reared Roger (rare striped possum) from a very young age for Worrals Park Zoo, NSW, to ascertain his diet requirements.
He lived in our bedroom

All the animals and birds, carefully packed with food, bedding, or perches, awaiting collection to go to Clandon Park Zoo in Miami.

Richard collecting animals from Papuans who sourced them, saving them from being eaten.

We bred Alpacas, and showed them.

Right and below: Richard loved the alpacas, and it was reciprocal.

7

Back in the 60s, Port Moresby was a very pleasant place in which to live. It was fringed with reefs and warm water lapping the white sandy beaches, leading on to coastal plains with undulating hills and valleys behind. True, it was hot, and sometimes very wet. It was what one expected in the tropics and measures were taken to alleviate the discomfort with sensible clothing, cool drinks and overhead fans.

It still had a bit of a frontier image about it, and appealed to people looking for adventure. It was served by ships coming up from Australia, like the *Bulolo*, *Malekula* or *Montoro*, but a lot came by air in turbo-prop aircraft thundering over Bootless Bay with flaps lowered, crossing the coast in a direct approach to Jackson's airport, above an emerald green-blue sea and outcrops of coral and white beaches below.

Upon leaving, two, five or ten years later, the same sight would be their last of a country they had either learned to love, possibly hate, but never to be indifferent about and always remember.

The newcomer would be a witness to the progress of an emerging country, a process started many years ago, belatedly some would say, but gaining impetus now due to internal and external pressures.

It's hard to analyse whether people change a country, or whether a country changes people. The tarmac, hot air fanning the face and a body clad in a close-fitting compress of normal clothes: the primary thought would be to change into tropical clothing. All other impressions of the airport activity, the mumble of voices, natives driving aircraft service utilities, dark faces lining guard rails, Customs officials and tropicalised Europeans, would be secondary to the need to get cool.

Shopping for necessities was a good introduction. It was a unique experience for a European, for the first time, to see the intermingling of white and dark people, which on the surface was quite amicable but there was the unspoken acceptance that the white man, the Taubada, was running the show.

There was a big selection of imported cheeses, smoked meat and salamis from Europe, exotic condiments and spices from Hong Kong, Indonesia and Malaysia, and caviar from the USSR. Within a short time, Moresby residents developed sophisticated tastes, and to tap this source, entrepreneurs were beginning to open up little restaurants with tasteful décor, air conditioning, a wine list, light music and good food. A big, new hotel and restaurant complex was being developed at the airport.

Progress was afoot, but many mourned the gradual disappearance of the old Territory establishments with their heavy cane chairs, rattan tables and overhead fans, and barefooted hotel employees wearing lap laps around their waists. For those with a penchant for nostalgia, a few such places still existed, where one could sit in somewhat seedy comfort in the company of unshaven gentry of various pursuits, newspaper correspondents, fishermen, traders and a few professional croc hunters.

The latter were nomads of the sea and inland rivers, away from the big smoke and following a life of adventure. We got to know one of them, a tall rangy New Zealander, a tough bloke, who came up to New Guinea in a self-built forty-foot yacht, leaving behind his job as an accountant . His rifles were the very best, made by W.J. Jeffrey in the UK, .404 in calibre, and the ammunition came from there too. He'd drift in the Papuan Gulf, silencing his engines, and slowly approach a big saltwater crocodile sunning itself on a floating palm tree and send a bullet down its throat. He had a couple of Papuan skinners whose job it was to jump in, secure the crocodile and subsequently skin it, ensuring no rips or slits in the belly skin. He would also navigate his way up narrow rivers, deep into the jungle, selling trinkets such as mirrors, scissors, small axes, needle and thread, matches et cetera. A lone traveller, communing with himself and whatever demons were in his soul. His exploits in Papua came to an end when the chief minister issued laws prohibiting unlimited crocodile hunting with licences required, so he moved down to Western Australia in the Broome and Kimberley coast area.

Following this decree, the wildlife section of the Department of Agriculture and Stock and Fisheries also began to take an interest in conservation, and instances of exploitation of resources, some of which were affecting local natives in remote areas. They took up the case of the Tonda people, who lived in the grasslands in the south-west corner of Papua, an area that held thousands of deer, mainly sambahs and cheetal, migrants from Dutch-held Hollandia, but previously from India. The deer were part of the diet of the Tondas.

Traders and others with business interest looked at the commercial aspects, planning to slaughter the deer and export the venison; also there was a plan to build a hunting lodge for tourists. The Tonda were not exactly averse to these plans, but were worried that the deer numbers would be depleted.

The department started issuing hunting permits and initiated a scheme to make sure that the tribe received royalties. It was a far-sighted appreciation that wildlife was an integral part of the traditional way of life, supplying protein, also for totems and sundry ornaments, horns as digging tools et cetera. It was also noted by extensive surveys that some native fauna such as cassowary, wild pig, goanna, tree kangaroo, wallaby, numerous species of cus cus and wild pigeon were on their way to extinction in some areas.

There was a time when a spear, a trap, a bow and arrow were adequate for a day's hunting. Patrol officers often reported that hunting parties regularly returned empty-handed. The shotgun was to blame. Villagers were calling for controls. Questionnaires were sent to all districts. In the majority of cases, the people gave their opinions, wondering what was happening to their animal and birdlife and the answer lay in the proliferation of shotguns. Single-barrel guns were allowed only for elders, and nominated hunters. There was an even greater threat: animals, pythons, birds of paradise, butterflies were being smuggled to overseas buyers who paid enormous sums.

The newcomer would find that within a few months the energy and well-being with which one arrived would tend to be dissipated by the unvarying heat, so that a sort of lethargy became apparent in movement and general behaviour. Most people at this stage began the precautionary measures of taking vitamin tablets and having citrus-type drinks, in addition of course to cold South Pacific beer, tepid showers and sleeping naked, legs apart under an overhead fan.

Gradually, a way of life would become the norm in which the whirring of fans was a constant factor, the refrigerator stacked with cold drinks and beer, locating the nearest shopping centre and the proximity of the Chinese trade store, the acceptance of noise from neighbours, and the desultory plucking of guitar strings from the boi-house.

Advice from neighbours would be the first source of information. How much to pay one's house-boi, and how to treat him. It was a good way to judge one's neighbour. Some would advocate a particular Chinese trade store run by Mr Wu, or Mrs Wong: while the prices of articles were inevitably higher, their convenience and quick service outweighed a longer trip to the regular shopping areas. It was also instructive to see how the Chinese treated natives: in general, curt, peremptory, devoid of kindness and respect. I suppose it would be the same way an Indian shopkeeper would treat a Kikuyu in Kenya. It was no wonder that when riots broke out, it was the trade store owners who bore the brunt.

The thrice-weekly newspaper provided a good coverage of Territory news, with politics inevitably taking precedence. There were the usual clarion calls for a climate of confidence and safeguards for business and industrial enterprises: the formation of new and impatient political parties, grumbling in the ranks of the Public Service, general criticism of Canberra and the Westminster system of government. It was valid to remember that the country, in its emergent role, was unique: there was not a single political prisoner, no one attempting to fast until death, no baton charges had been made and no shots echoed in the streets.

Tribal conflicts in remote areas, particularly in the Highlands in the Chimbu and Goilala areas, were regularly reported, describing sorties from one hill to another. Death by axe, spear and arrow generally invited revenge, the payback, and the law was hard put to persuade relatives of the victims to accept the white man's penalty of five years in Bomana prison for the guilty party, to the more traditional and satisfying one of a spear through the ribs, a cassowary thighbone dagger through the armpit or an axe chop on the neck.

These regular incidents were sent down to the Australian papers through the medium of Morse code and to achieve brevity, a special type of journalese was adopted in which a fracas in the mountains would be reduced to 'five Chimbus deathwards arrow-wise'.

Some of the sentences meted out appeared lenient. The judge took into account the relative degree of sophistication of the tribesmen. The urban native tended to collect a stiffer sentence than someone recently emerged from the bush. Misdemeanours, such as bar fights, peeping into girls' dormitories, shoplifting, housebreaking and hitting umpires were commonplace and kept the police fully occupied.

There was another magazine, *Black and White*, with iconoclastic tendencies that appeared once a month. It had little to say that was original but fed on items from elsewhere. Sometimes, it hit the nail on the head and created discussions on some aspect of Territory life which evoked popular dissent. Its language was crude, and it was blatantly racist: it promoted the idea that natives were close relatives of Neanderthal man, having recently swung down from the trees. In the main, having nothing constructive to say, it deplored all actions of government, criticised Europeans and natives alike, and it was a measure of tolerance in the Territory that it was quite eagerly sought after. It also had a comic strip in which heroes, Matt Mekeo in particular, and villains always wore tufts of grass, fore and aft, and the hero would be urged to 'Go for his arse-grass'. One publication went too far in its criticism of a prominent government minister and its licence was revoked. Copies of the paper are now collector's items.

With the passage of time, the newcomer would find that many preconceived notions and ideas would be whittled away by an imperceptible process, and adaption towards a Territory way of thinking would begin. It was generally accepted that five years would have to elapse before the process was complete, by which time one would be admitted into the ranks of the Territorians True: a term which could have various meanings. Some had a totally colonial attitude, that of the white man over the brown, nurturing feelings of distrust and attitudes bordering on apartheid. There were others who over time surrendered all disciplined values previously held and slowed themselves down to what were considered the more indolent, native pace and attitudes, and at the other end of the spectrum were some who with missionary zeal involved themselves in the local culture, learned the language and ceaselessly fostered tolerance between races, spending many years in their pursuits.

In the mid-60s, Port Moresby had a population of approximately 45,000, of which 12,000 were European or of Asian heritage. Like any town of similar size, it had its tradesmen, businessmen, bank clerks, civil servants and educationalists. The class structure of Australian society was perpetuated here and, by example and close association, began to influence Papuans who took up employment in the various trades, with the end product being a class structure which had an educated elite on one side, the garbage disposal teams on the other and tradesmen and public service clerks in the middle, all held together by an acceptance of necessary discipline. It became apparent that while Australia was occupying the seat of government, the status quo would remain, but when the country gained independence, it would have to rely on its own discipline, and of course maintain the will to do so.

The average Papuan was constantly learning from the example set by the average European resident, and whether the latter was conscious of it or not, he was an ambassador of his country. Few Europeans ever tried to see out their three score and ten in the Territory. Australians, New Zealanders and others came up on two- or three-year contracts, seeking higher wages and a bit of a change in a tropical setting. When their term was over, they departed, leaving very little – perhaps the lawns and trees they'd planted. A few residents led exemplary lives and passed on the benefits of their knowledge, but for most, the sum total of their achievement was a couple of thousand in the bank, a suntan, a smattering of Pidgin or Motu, a thirst for South Pacific beer, and memories of the coral trout and red emperors they'd caught on the reefs.

For the newcomer, learning to be patient was very necessary. The native clerk behind the post office counter did his best to meet requests: his mental arithmetic was better than average, but haste was not an inherent part of his make-up. A few years ago, he was a pot-bellied village boy in a bush hut, struggling to learn English. The fact that he had mastered a foreign tongue and passed his examinations was proof enough of his intelligence.

There were thousands like him, employed through the structure of government. They were the first generation of Papuans and New Guineans to emerge with the advantages of a good basic education. It was this generation, under the umbrella of the Australian School of Pacific Administration that was acquiring university degrees, undergoing teacher training and replacing Europeans, forming trade unions and political parties. There were signs of impatience, not only with the dictates being channelled up from Canberra, but with their own elders in government, men of a more cautious and conservative bent, and of different tribal elements, whom the youngsters considered too amenable and subservient.

Speedy jet travel, a growing population and the efforts of the tourist board had combined to make Moresby a place worth visiting. Visiting pianists and violinists played to enthusiastic audiences. The German Tubigen had made a tremendous impression, but when the Royal Australian Ballet performed *Giselle*, it drew whoops and thigh slapping from the natives on the front grassy mound when they saw tall, young white ballerinas in tutus being held aloft and transported at shoulder height, exposing their thighs and undergarments, which was quite embarrassing for the appreciative and reserved white audience.

There was always plenty to do. Excursions to Sogeri, where the rubber country starts, with a whole networks of narrow tracks beyond, leading towards Kokoda. A winding climb up to the range to Rouna Falls and the Rouna Hotel. Swimming at Idlers Bay, and for the more intrepid, there was scuba diving off Basilisk beacon, and the dark depths.

The reefs off Moresby were a fisherman's paradise: trolling with Smith's jigs off the main reef between the wreck of the Pruth and Basilisk, or bottom fishing for red emperor in the deep waters of Bootless Bay.

There were large swamps around Moresby, teeming with wild duck, and tributaries off the Brown River feeding the swamps and allowing barramundi and black bass to enter. Conditions were difficult and fraught with the annoyance of millions or mosquitos, numerous snakes, and of course the lurking menace of crocodiles.

Moresby was like a state of its own, set apart and not quite typical of the Territory as a whole. Residents in the mountains up in Mt Hagen and Goroka, or those further away in Rabaul and Kavieng, would say, in a derogatory sense, that Moresby was just an extension of Queensland.

Perhaps, but behind the lapping blue sea and reefs and the low undulating hills covered in grassland, Moresby was an outpost: just half an hour's flight away, there were dense jungles and razor-backed almost inaccessible mountains shrouded in mist, and down in the valleys were primitive people, some only recently brought within government jurisdiction. Moresby had a beautiful harbour, a modern town and neat suburbs, natives and Europeans going about their business in a, so far, law-abiding township, and it was from here that the whole fascinating land was governed, and the people who lived in its confines tended to be proud of the place.

I was still a hunter. I couldn't see a bird flying without tracking it with an imaginary gun barrel, leading it by the required amount and expelling my breath in a simulated discharge of the shot, and then mentally recording a hit or a miss.

With the passage of time, one begins to question oneself. The urge to hunt was still a part of me but it was no longer an imperative.

Before I reformed, some friends and I formed a regular hunting group, heading for the swamps perhaps every six weeks or so. One of the party had a Toyota Land Cruiser. Loaded to the gunwales with guns, ammunition, mosquito nets and repellent, fishing nets and rods, plus a zinc-lined trunk full of ice, we'd head north. Skirting Fairfax Harbour, we'd go through an area of savannah, undulating terrain with low hills covered in kunai grass, up past Papa and Lea Lea on the coast and then turn inland to meet the area where the Waigani and Doura Swamps joined. The former was an area of about 160 square miles, a huge permanent swamp and gathering place for thousands of waterfowl, feeding on the lush growth. The Brown River, which fed the swamp, also gave it predatory barramundi and bass hunters who nosed their way in searching for tarpon and tilapia.

The natives who lived in villages bordering the swamps had no problems meeting their protein requirements. They'd select a prong of the swamp, fairly narrow and tapering, ideal for driving fish into. The entire village population would take part, with lots of shouting and enthusiasm. A thirty-metre net would block the end and the wading mass of bodies would drive the fish in. Literally tons of fish would be caught, the flapping bodies being scooped up into baskets ready to be taken to Koki market, leaving more than enough for village consumption. They jealously guarded their territory, including their banana groves and the surrounding savannah where wallaby roamed.

We were challenged when we first went in, but the gift of some twelve-gauge shotgun shells plus our earnest comments that we were careful people, respecting their area, not intent on destroying it, was sufficient to build up a rapport. On subsequent trips, we'd meet the headman and always gave him a box of twenty-five shotgun cartridges. We were scrupulous in our dealings: if we helped ourselves to bananas, we left money under a stone, and it was the same when we came across their sweet potatoes, pumpkins and other gourds.

It was a long way from Moresby just for a day's hunting, so we asked the headman for permission to erect a timber and galvanised-iron hut.

He was agreeable and over a period of several months material was carried in to make a fairly substantial, weatherproof hut of about six by four metres. In it we put our camp beds, boxes, forty-four-gallon drums of water and fuel, cartridge belts, axes, fishing rods, the lot. Not a single item was touched by the natives.

It was comfortable and a haven, but nothing could stop the mosquitos. It was a case of applying more repellent, or sitting in a deliberate smoke-filled room, inhaling and coughing. We were now able to come out for a few days. The place was teeming with duck and their mutterings could be heard all night. Whistling teal were there in their thousands and as a flock flew over it was possible to literally just point the gun upwards and without looking to pull the trigger and bring down two or three birds. Flocks milled around in the sky above us in a sort of turmoil with flapping wings and cries from thousands of throats. Very rapidly, we became selective, shooting only for the pot, bringing down mainly high, fast-flying black ducks. We had learnt earlier that the more we shot, the more work had to be done, more water to be boiled, birds to be gutted and feathers to be plucked.

It was on one of the earlier occasions that I brought down two whistlers. I could see that they were winged as they tumbled and then planed down to splash into the water about twenty metres from me. They disappeared immediately. The water was very shallow, less than half a metre, and I waded out expecting them to bob up at my feet: but no, they'd hit the water and then swum off at a tangent, just like partridges do on land. Up they popped further on, down they went, up and down, and over a ten-minute period I quartered back and forth. I felt remorse and wanted to catch them, feeling that I could repair the damage inflicted. I went back to the edge and put my gun against a tree and then waded back in. I chased them here and there and was led a merry dance, soaked to the skin as the water splashed up at me. I could see them, like torpedoes, streamlined, darting around.

I tried another tactic and stood absolutely still and let the water settle and then I saw one, a cunning little devil. Using its beak, it was grasping some weeds on the swamp floor, holding its breath, but for how long? I came closer, very quietly and when in range I scooped it up and, holding it under my arm, I searched and found the other. I held them both to my chest, full of guilt. I'd brought them down from the sky, on a whim. They were soft and dappled brown, wet feathers and glistening beaks, lovely curves to their necks. Their soft brown eyes looked into mine: they seemed to say, why? I said hello and told them I was sorry. I truly was. At the end of that particular shoot, I took them home, put them in a large, safe run, dug a pond for them and made them comfortable. They were named Tony and Tammy.

I was a sinner, frequently repentant, but yet could not resist the urge to hunt. A charge from the choke barrel speeding towards an angling fast-flying black resulted in an instantaneous death, and this by some convoluted logic made it not so bad. There was even some elation when there were two blacks and both were brought down with a left and right barrel.

Regrettably, that's exactly what happened on one occasion. The nearest was about ten metres away and I was thigh deep in a weedy patch of water when I picked it up. I fixed it to my belt and moved further out to get the other one, slowly pushing through the weeds waist deep and was just about to reach out when there was a hit against my thigh, a heavy push of water against me, a swirl and the duck vanished. My mind raced. Croc!! I had visions of thrusting the gun barrel down into the jaws that would crush my waist and of pulling the trigger, if I had time. Of course there would be no time. Grabbed and pulled under in a flash and then rolled over and over. I pushed my way out of the water in a panic.

It was incidents like that and the sight of snakes all over the place that, while producing that exhilarating pull of danger causing the adrenalin to flow did, nevertheless, exact its toll. It was the day after we'd returned to Moresby, having survived the hostile environment, that massive post-tension headaches and nightmares would result. I often wondered whether it was worth it, until the next time a few weeks later and we'd be off again. Annette was very worried. She knew that hunting was in my blood but my headaches and the dangers I'd described were giving her sleepless nights, wondering what could happen to me. I decided to do the right thing. I spoke to my mates and said I was going to pack it in. It was too dicey. They agreed that we'd all had close shaves and they too would possibly pull back a bit.

We must have had charmed lives. We'd spend literally all day in the water, varying from areas just ankle-deep where one could actually shoot fleeing tilapia, aiming just ahead of the bow wave as the school fled into deeper water, but mostly it was in thigh- or waist-deep stretches, making slow progress against a thick, restraining barrier of weeds wrapped around one's middle, stopping to push it down, stepping over and, leaning forward, start again. We were at our most vulnerable when at shoulder depth, chins up, just clearing the water, gun barrel outstretched trying to tap and pull in a fallen bird. It was madness.

I had two close shaves with snakes. I was fishing for tilapia, standing at the edge of a body of water, casting in and minding my own business when I heard a sharp hiss and felt a thump against the ankle of my boot. I quickly looked down to see a metre-long brown snake turning and retreating at speed. Another time, I was stalking a mob of pygmy geese, crouching low and taking slow deliberate steps, eyes on the flock, when I trod on the tail of a Papuan black. Up he rose, turning to strike, when I lifted my foot and he took off. It all happened in less than half a second.

There were small channels running from the river into the swamps, some barely five metres wide and possibly two metres deep, and it was hard to credit that big barramundi would be moving silently in and out. We'd set a net early in the evening, return to the hut for dinner, a few drinks, sitting around a fire and plucking ducks that had been dunked in a boiling forty-four-gallon drum. At about eleven p.m., we'd head for the nets and, sure enough, the big corks would be bobbing. It was on these nocturnal forays that we'd see a lot of snakes, and the whole area was full of danger. Under torch and kerosene lantern light, we'd haul the net in. It was not unusual to find seven or eight barra of fifteen to twenty kilos each, and holes in the net where bigger fish had expanded their gills and cut their way through. We'd do another set and collect more fish in the morning.

8

Young Richard had gone past the crawling stage and was now on his feet, still a bit unsteady but smiling happily as he came down the passageway holding the toilet brush in his hand, in much the same way as a tightrope walker holds a pole to maintain his balance. He liked pushing the toilet brush into the toilet to hear the water splash and his fascination for that area drew him later to chuck my entire pay packet into the bowl. Pay in those days, came fortnightly in a brown envelope. He was happily independent, but we felt that he needed a companion, and subsequently his little sister, Karen, was born to keep him company.

We still had Tanya and Tramp, our dogs, Tatters and Tosca, the birds, Taiyuan and Thomas, the cats, Tallulah the lizard, Tony and Tammy, ducks, and large as life Timothy, the agile wallaby. He was now full grown, prone to wandering, and needed a mate.

We wrote to the owner of Worrel's zoo and reptile park at Gosford in New South Wales. It was a magnificent zoo holding not only Australian animals but also New Guinea mammals, and reptiles of every sort. It was the only place in Australia where poisonous snakes and spiders were milked for their venom, the product going to the Commonwealth Serum Laboratory for processing into antivenene to counter the effects of snake bites from brown snakes, red-bellied blacks, taipans, vipers and funnel web spiders. We asked him if he would accept Timothy, and offered ourselves as conduits for animals that we knew were sent to him from many areas of Papua and New Guinea, mainly from planters up in the Highlands. A letter came back accepting our offer and I set about making arrangements, which were the construction of a crate, a permit to export, a vet certificate and, most importantly, the manner of transport.

Fortunately some of the China Navigation ships were still visiting Moresby and other ports and the skipper of the *Chungking* was a friend of mine from the good old days. When I knew him, he was a second mate. Also, the radio officer onboard used to be my number two. The skipper readily agreed to take Timothy down to Sydney and the crate was lifted by a crane and safely placed in a sheltered spot on deck, along with adequate water and food. He was going to a good home.

About ten days later, we received word from Worrel's that Timothy was enjoying his new surroundings. A week after that, we got news that Timothy was having a ball and, being allowed free ranging, had found his way into the kitchens. He had scattered pots and pans everywhere, upturned barrels of flour and bowls of cooling proodge. He was up to his old tricks. He was caught and shunted off to a separate paddock, free to roam.

At the same time, we received a request from Peter Krauss the curator of the zoo, who was also its expert snake handler, whether we could possibly put him up in our spare room and help him in his snake catching activities by driving him around. We immediately agreed and I was particularly excited at the prospect of seeing him in action.

He came up a few months later and brought his Finnish wife with him, Raija, a lovely-looking woman; she only stayed for a few days and then flew home, happy with her brief glimpse of PNG life. Peter was very patient while waiting for my off-work periods. During our daytime sorties, we drove down the Rigo Road in savannah country, stopping at derelict, abandoned huts, fallen timber, rusting iron sheeting, old rainwater tanks. Several snakes were caught by surprise as a sheet of tin was removed and Peter in a quick action leaned forward in a quick fluid movement catching behind the head: no hesitant, tentative motions was the secret. He carried small cloth bags made by Annette with a double seam, into which he fed the snakes and closed the drawstrings. Large spiders, the size of tarantulas, were simply caught by dropping a handkerchief-sized cloth over them.

Night time was the best. We'd drive down the Laloki, Brown River,

Vanapa Road, in the area where Annette and I had been lost in the jungle several years ago, and with the headlights on we'd come across snakes crossing the road every five minutes or so. I'd stop, Peter would get out and quite nonchalantly approach the reptile, simply stoop down and pick it up, as easy as pie. The glare of the headlights evidently bamboozled them.

He stayed a fortnight and in that time he had forty-three snakes, hanging in calico bags which Annette also made, ensuring the snakes couldn't find a hole by doing a double stitch called a French seam.

A trader, known to Worrel from previous times, sent down three olive pythons and four amethysts, all in the three- to four-metre range. They came down from Baimuru in a Steamships coastal freighter, secure in gunny sacks. This consignment, along with two amethysts that Peter had caught near the Vanapa River where I had driven him, plus half the consignment already in calico bags hanging up in our garage, were to be equally shared between Worrel and Stuttgart Zoo, the curator of which was a friend of Peter's. One of the olive pythons had an ulcerated lower jaw and I regularly helped Peter to hold the snake while he used tweezers to pull away rotting flesh, applying ointment and flushing the wound with diluted Dettol. It took all of our collective strength to hold it firmly while it writhed, throwing its coils over our arms and on one occasion around Peter's neck. It was during one of these occasions that as he looked into the tea chest, the snake hurled itself upwards, jaws agape and struck him in the face: the fangs of the top jaw were embedded in his skull just above the left eyebrow and the partially fangless bottom jaw punctured his cheek. We managed to pull it off. He was quite calm about it, accepting it as one of the hazards of the job. It took a while for the bleeding to stop and the punctures were cleaned with Dettol, and some antiseptic powder was applied. He had a swollen cheek for the next few days.

At about this time, I developed a case of mumps. I had fever and periods of delirium and was quite ill for a while. I lost one testicle. Tests were conducted and I was assured that I had enough tadpoles for further procreation. That year, Annette became pregnant and a little girl named Kylie was born. We now had our hands full. Procreation was easy in PNG, what with hot nights and lying naked under whirring fans.

Before the preparation for another shipment, Peter brought up the subject again of sending Tosca, the eclectus, and the two whistlers to Stuttgart. We agreed to his request but made a proviso that because Tosca was a house pet, she should be treated the same way in Stuttgart and not housed in some vast aviary. This was agreed upon and we decided to do so just before we left Port Moresby.

It was a busy time preparing the crates for shipment. Peter had also acquired two phalanger maculatus maculatus arboreal mammals, which regrettably had a fight in their cage, with one receiving a large gash in its side. In true bush doctor style, he used needle and fishing line to suture the flaps of the wound together and added a bit of antiseptic, and it was enough to allow air travel.

The pythons actually gave no trouble in being handled into their tea chests in their bags. The first python was fed into the bottom of the chest and immediately a sheet of plywood was placed over it, an exact fit, then the next reptile and another sheet, and so on until six pythons were in situ and the lid was nailed down. It was quite creepy to see the tea chest bulge, expand and contract as each snake shuffled itself into a comfortable position, ready for its flight to Germany. It was also quite amusing to see the reaction of the native airport staff as they witnessed the movements from inside the chest when they were called to lift it, which required at least three men.

While Peter was with us, I received a note from a tea planter up in the Highlands, saying that a consignment of snakes were on their way, with a cryptic comment saying, 'Be careful of these boigas.' Peter knew what they were: finger-thin, green tree snakes, as fast as lightning. They were housed in a narrow wooden box in which there were three dowels, and wrapped around the dowels were about a dozen boigas. They were writhing around, heads up and snapping at each other.

Peter grabbed one, then another, and pulled them free of the dowel and then bang, one got him on the thumb, and then like lightning another got him on the side of his palm. 'Oops!' he said, shut the lid and sucked both bite areas. 'Not poisonous,' he added and then continued pulling them out, tucking them into their bags.

Peter went back down south after sending the shipment off and said he'd be back in a few months, and in the interim could we hold the fort and be a conduit for further animals. We agreed. In due course, we received a young male tree kangaroo from the gentleman who'd sent us the boigas. He added in his note that he was sending down a pound of his tea with his daughter Tina, which was very decent of him. He also hoped that we were successful with the sugar gliders from Tufi. We had received them earlier, a tight-knit family of about seven members, and all were doing well in their cage in our garage.

We couldn't help ourselves: on one of our bush trips, we saw a white cus cus, a maculatus maculatus, confined to a tiny cage, destined for the cooking pot. We bought it and it joined the merry throng. We called her Feety.

About a month previously, we had received a white female cus cus from a gentleman in Madang who, with humanitarian feelings similar to ours, had bought the animal from a native. It was in a very neglected state and he was sure it would become a stew in due course. He cared for it and brought it back to good health. The diet, apart from all sorts of fruit, was supplemented by baby cereal mixed with sweetened condensed milk and water to a porridge consistency.

Two more tree kangaroos arrived from the Highlands but on the very next day one of them had a fit, thrashing around, and died a few minutes later, which was rather sad. I decapitated it and put the head in a formalin solution, tightly sealed in a plastic bag. I knew that heads were needed for study purposes, dental structure et cetera.

It was getting quite hectic and we were beginning to feel the strain. Apart from visits to the airport to pick up animals sent down from Highland sources, there were also animals from the Gulf, all from sources that Peter had found. We had to house them, feed them, arrange vet certificates, export permits and shipment by sea, all very time consuming. Following his last visit, we sent down four wallabies, four cus cus and two possums to be housed in the Taronga Park facility for a thirty-day period.

We had long ago learnt the native names for the animals we sought, identification of which was assisted by PNG postage stamps which featured fauna and flora of the Territory. Cus cus was vagula or voura. Bandicoot – mora. Echidna – moragini or modagini. And sugar gliders – diro diro.

The scientific names were inserted with all shipments. spotted cus cus was Phalanger Maculatus Maculatus. We had several cus cus, or Phalangers, Orientalis, Maculatus Goldei, Atrimaculatus, Gymnotis and Vestitus, the names varying according to their range, such as northwest New Guinea, Papua, or around Madang and Hollandia, some at sea level and others from high altitude. Sugar gliders were Petaurus Brebiceps and echidnas were Tachyglossus Aculeatus. It was all quite confusing ut we managed.

9

We were now almost a quarter of the way through our ninth year in Moresby. Our plan was to call it a day at the end of the year. We were tired. Also, young Richard and Karen were at the stage where they were happily barefooted, a pair of shorts around their waists, their little bodies tanned by the sunshine, and Kylie was crawling faster and faster. Naomi, our haus meri, wife of Jacob, our haus boi, doted on them. Jacob was a Mumeng from the Lae area whom we had employed after Qualim departed, despite protests from the Rigo mob. He and Naomi were excellent. Naomi had given birth to a little daughter whom she named Annette.

It was time the kids were exposed to the outer world. In fact, their early toddler days were not dissimilar to mine, way back in India with caring, indulgent servants. Our plans, still being formulated, were to make a pilgrimage back to India to show Annette and the kids where I was born, the house in which I lived and the school I went to up in the Himalayas, including the dormitory and the corner where my bed had been situated. The rivers I swam in, floating down seated on the back of a buffalo, the football field where leopards could be seen in the moonlight. From there, on to Greece, then on to England to stay with my sister, and part of the dream was to possibly hire or even buy a camping wagon in which to tour England, then across to central Europe. Over the years, we'd been doing a bit of saving and the enterprise of animal collecting had added some. There was hope.

Then a semi-miracle happened, the implementation of which could augment the sum required: there was a gradual dawning in our ruminations that if we accepted the path being offered, then all our hopes could be realised.

My eldest brother, Arthur, lived in Fort Lauderdale, Florida. He was now an American citizen, married, with his own architectural business, and by one of the quirks of fate it happened as stories develop, page by page. A German torpedo sank his ship, the *Eclipse*, off the coast of Florida, in 1942. The crew were rescued and taken ashore. In Lauderdale, he met a girl, Mary, fell in love and got married in a fortnight. He was then repatriated to England. At the end of the war, he returned to Lauderdale, where he studied and became an architect. His close friend was superintendent of Crandon Park Zoo, Miami.

When the superintendent heard that Arthur had a brother in Papua who was interested in the native animals, it raised his interest and he asked Arthur to contact me with a view to getting together a collection of New Guinea animals. Letters went back and forth and, in spite of knowing we had a huge task ahead of us, we agreed, mainly because we didn't want to disappoint Arthur. The request was for phalangers of all types, bandicoots, dorcopsis wallabies, echidnas, sugar gliders, and crocodile heads with skin still attached. A large shipment. We asked that a formal request should be made to the Deparrment of Agriculture, Stock and Fisheries. Government of Papua New Guinea, stipulating the type of marsupial and nominating me as an official animal collector. This was done, approval was given and the real hard work started.

Over a period of several years, we had made notes of road conditions, attitudes of the inhabitants of the villages we had visited, their general reliability and if there were any hostile intimations. We followed the ground rules carefully. If by accident we happened to run over a fowl or a pig near a village, we were advised to ignore the natural urge to stop and to continue on our way as fast as possible. The Papuans could often be belligerent, and when surrounded by an angry mob, the outcome could be unfortunate.

When we made contact with people in any village, Annette and I always presented ourselves as being friendly, using small phrases we had picked up in Pidgin and Motu, and always kept promises we made. If we said we'd come back on Thursday next week, we'd move heaven and earth to do that. There were times when we'd see villagers in a cluster at the base of a hut and assess their attitude towards us. Their faces gave nothing away, totally expressionless except for the furtive scrutiny through generally bloodshot eyes at the white man in front of them. After showing them postage stamps depicting the animals we were after, and how many we wanted, we'd wait for a response. We could almost visualise the gears working in their minds, meshing and unmeshing, slowly working things out, and at last one of them would nod. It was all we could expect.

When we returned on the appointed day, in all probability we'd find the same group, in the same position, almost as if they hadn't moved a muscle. Expressing no visual disappointment, we'd offer a smile and say we'd come back, same time next week. As it happened, on many occasions after the first two visits, we'd return to find several hessian sacks lying in a row, holding animals. We'd give an animated display of joy and pay immediately and respond to the usual mutter to 'Go Moresby kwik taim em e no gat kai kai na warrer.' In other words, they had been captured, secured and subdued, with no food or water. We'd head for Moresby quick time.

All of this was being accomplished while being fully occupied with communications work which entailed a six week spell of duty in the town office where Morse and teleprinter traffic came in and went out in a more or less continual stream. The traffic load was tremendous. We lived with Morse in our ears, hammering into our brains. We were professional radio officers and formed a sort of elite group, selected for Port Moresby based on our ability to handle the stressful situations that were ever present. It was relentless. Just when the last bundle of messages were sent down the chute, there'd be a pause, just enough to roll a cigarette, when another wad would come down in a thump, or if there was no pause, we were adept enough to let a blistering stream of Morse whiz by, containing about a dozen words, memorise them, roll the cigarette and then go like the clappers to add the words and pick up the ongoing stream.

Sometimes we punched so fast we could beat the machines. Sweat trickled down our ribs. There was no air conditioning. No toilet in the building. Meagre facilities. A basin and a tap, just enough for tea making. Then when we thought we had a break, in would come the press corps with thousands of words more. We who shared the load in the town office were aware of a bond between us, based on mutual respect for the ability to work under continual stress, heat and generally unbearable conditions. There were times when I'd end a shift with a visible tremor in my hands, aware that if I had a day off, Annette and I would be way down the Vanapa River Road or somewhere, keeping a promise to come and pick up an animal, or go to the airport and collect specimens there.

After six weeks in the town office, there would be a six week spell in the communications building on the other side of the airport, way over on the perimeter surrounded by tall kunai grass, and at night an island of light in a desolate of sea of darkness. It was a blessed relief from the town office but was certainly no rest cure. All coastal shipping and incoming ocean-going vessels listened to our weather reports, checked in on our regular schedules, gave their daily positions: we monitored the safety of life at sea frequencies channel 16 VHF, 2182 khz, and 500 khz on medium frequency. Here we controlled massive CY10 transmitters. We were still visited by the press when the town office was shut and when urgent press was needed down south to meet deadlines. The station closed at eleven p.m. and it was a lonely drive back home. It wasn't far from a Goilala encampment and it was often that some of them, after leaving the last tavern to come to the plate glass, flatten their noses against the glass, almost Neanderthal in appearance and stare in, totally uncomprehending. Though the place was bolted and barred, I always had a .22 rifle beside the console.

A typical day off appeared in my diary as:

Worked. Prepared cases, painted. Made dozens of phone calls. Qantas checking on onward bookings. Checked with Papuan Agents. Rang Health and got vet to inspect animals. Wrote to Dr Gordon. Got to bed at 2 a.m.

(Drove to Boregaina. Village apparently deserted in blazing afternoon heat. Quaint Samoan type church, up on stilts. Awoke an old Catholic priest from his afternoon sleep and asked for animals. None, he said. People too hungry and all animals used for food. Persevered and found a man, David, who showed me an orientalis cus cus in a cage under the eaves. Offered him $2 to come in the car with me and find the owner. Tracked him from block to block. Found him but he said his son is back in the village. Time now 5 p.m. and Moresby 100 miles away. Found the son, Dagira, who agreed to sell the animal for $10. Relieved to see she was a female and would be a mate for Horace our male orientalis. Drove back to Moresby at high speed. Got home)

Shift work for the next two days, then heard that a tree kangaroo would be arriving at the airport from the Highlands. Rushed to Steamships to get a couple of tea chests. Prepared cages. In bed at 2 a.m.

And again when I drove home, my mind was on when and where I'd head for the next day.

We were still getting animals from the Highlands and shipping them down to Worrell's, with all the attendant laborious paperwork, and now, with shrinking time constraints in view of our departure from Papua, the pressure was on us. Our collection for Miami zoo was growing.

I extracted all my notes, compiled over the years.

Animal sources. MOITAKA. I don't know exactly where from in Moitaka but a young native lad, named Peter, a rare find in that he was able to converse in a smattering of English arrived with two female orientalis cus cus: he heard on the grapevine that we would be coming on this particular day. We were very pleased. When asked if he could get a male he showed complete confidence in being able to do so. A week later when we visited he was there with a healthy male. Several of his relatives were also there in a Moitaka Estate utility truck, painted blue. He also had a young Torres Strait pigeon with him, but in the general excitement of getting the male orientalis the bird escaped.

LALOKI TRADE STORE (Operated by a Mr. Large). Nearly all vehicular traffic using the Kuriva-Vanapa-Brown River Road stops at the store, and he reports seeing echidnas, bandicoots and the occasional cus cus being taken to market. He gave me his telephone number and expressed a willingness to purchase and hold animals for us. He is also useful for passing messages down the line.

NEBIRI QUARRY ROAD. About 300 yards down this road beyond the Laloki Trade Store there's a native material house on stilts with a disused red Holden utility nearby. An old man named Hepe lives here and is a source for dorcopsis wallabis. He is related to the Vikabu people beyond the Brown River bridge.

HAIMA VILLAGE. Turn off before Gill's Mountain View Estate. These people live in Savannah type country and can be tapped as a source for Agile wallabies and bandicoots. Arrangements can be made with the Gill's for the Haima people to bring their catches to them, and for contact to be made.

SABUSA SAWMILL. There's a small village just behind the sawmill. It's well situated, on the border of savannah and forest country and could be an excellent source. The contact here is a youth named Eugene, who speaks a bit of English. Acquired 3 dorcopsis wallabies.

VIKABU. About 6 miles beyond the Brown River bridge: it is ideally situated beside a fast flowing creek, spanned by a small bridge. The approach to the village is marked by a series of thick, white-painted posts. The contact is Gabrielle, a pleasant English speaking youth who appears to have the virtue of energy, coupled with a sense of honour. He really tried hard and over a period of time supplied 6 peroryctes raffrayanus bandicoots, 4 little dorcopsis forest wallabies and 1 tachyglossus aculeatus (echidna). Animal life seems to be abundant in the forest surrounding the village.

Two hundred yards beyond Vikabu – a small hamlet of two houses, one bordering the road and one set further back. Very clean with flowers planted everywhere, also an extensive sweet potato patch (kau kau). These people have gardens in forest clearings nearby. The rear house is owned by a well rounded, middle aged, moustached, English speaking and prosperous market gardener. He owns a jeep, a shotgun and has a pack of hunting dogs. He had four echidnas just a week before we contacted him and had disposed of them at the Koki market. We had more success with vegetables from him than animals, but he's a good potential source.

After this there is an unpopulated stretch of about five miles, then a series of small hamlets appear on the left hand side of the road, immediately followed by a large village which extends on both sides of the road. Wallabies can be obtained from them but not much else.

VANAPA RIVER VILLAGE. This side of the bridge. The contact here is Makena, a professional hunter and an excellent source. He'll get you anything you want, including crocodiles. He has an involuntary nervous twitch of his eyelids and can be easily recognised. He knows his area well. Unfortunately the crocodile heads we enquired about would not be suitable for Dr. Gordon, coming from small crocs no more than a metre and a half in length. We got numerous bandicoots and wallabies from him, and also the unidentified psuedocheirus possum from him. He supplies Koki market with a substantial share of its dorcopsis meat.

Two hundred yards further the road dips into a sawmill area. At the far end beside the riverbank there's a house occupied by Au, brother of Makena who is also a hunter and together these two are the best source in the Vanapa area. Au works for the Kuriva sawmill and has contact with the Kuriva people from whom animals can also be procured. In fact, after Vikabu all villages can be bypassed and collection can be left solely to Au and Makena.

DABUNARI VILLAGE. 21 mile: about 200 yards this side of Mrs Hickey's Trade Store, 300 yards off the road to the left. Contact here is the hunter, Kaia Beia. He hunts in the foothills about 3 hours walking distance from the village. Given good weather and 3 days to do his searching he can bring out cus cus, or any animal common to that area. Got a beautiful adult female maculatus cus cus from him. (A no nonsense lady. Haughty and imperious with eyes that didn't blink when looking at you. A banana held out would disappear in a blur as her slashing right arm took it from you. She had a ruff covering her throat and shoulders. We named her Victoria Rex). Kaia Beia has relatives in Wai Wai village and is sometimes located there.

DABODA AND SENONA VILLAGES. 28 to 36 mile mark. Each village has its hunter and both villages are well situated for Savannah animals. The contact at Senona is a young girl named Kakaira, who speaks schoolgirl English and acts as an interpreter.

KAPAKAPA TURN OFF. 50 yards to the right there's a small hamlet. A brindled bandicoot was obtained from here. About a mile further on there are two villages straddling the road: these people are quite keen. Obtained several isodons macrourous – brown brindled bandicoot, different from the raffyaranus, and an echidna from them.

A mile further there's Broadview Estate owned by the Modra family. About 300 yards past this there's a dirt road leading to the left. It continues 6 miles further to Gunagau village. The contact here is Tau Bou, who if given a definite order will provide animals. Good country.

KWIKILA. Mrs. Modra's Trade Store. A very pleasant, helpful and honest lady. She can contact the Garisi and Gair people and their hunters can catch any animal required.

At a more leisurely period and long before the urgency of animal collecting, we had had the foresight to buy many empty tea chests and converted them to contain the animals that we obtained, modifying many, adding hinged doors and wire mesh. Also some came in cages made out of native materials, fairly substantial and many still carrying traces of soot indicating that the poor creatures had been housed in the beams not far from the fire below. Our garage was beginning to fill up…again!

We bought a further twenty tea chests from Steamships and hired a local carpenter to modify them, sometimes dividing the chest into two compartments, for smaller animals, and even into four compartments for the sugar gliders and bandicoots. Empty kerosene tins were also acquired for the transport of echidnas. Echidnas love white ants and during our travels we located several huge white ant colonies, extending a several metres up from ground level and having scores of tunnels leading from the surface down into the cool bowels of the earth. Our shipping method was to break open a mound, shovel the earth and ants into a bag, empty the bag into the kerosene tin, place the echidna inside, close the lid, solder it tight and puncture breathing holes in the top. The method proved itself later when all the echidnas arrived in good shape.

All the cages were painted red and numbered. Time was running out and we redoubled our efforts. We began naming our charges.

Occupying our minds constantly was the thought that we had to make arrangements for household pets, members of our family to be looked after when we left the Territory, particularly the dogs Tanya and Tramp. We were hoping it would be so and were very relieved when our next-door neighbours agreed at once to look after them. As things turned out, there was an incident that might have made this unnecessary: Annette suffered some whiplash when the car was hit in the rear near Badili by a Papuan in a beat-up utility. 'Sori, no gat brake!' he apologised, 'Sori, sori.' The damage to the bumper bar was minor but for a few days Annette seemed rather vague and lethargic. Nevertheless, a few days later, she took the children to Ela Beach for a romp on the beach, along with Tanya and Tramp. Other friends also brought their children.

When I came home that evening after finishing my shift, I wanted to give the dogs their evening meal but couldn't find them. Annette was in bed and suddenly realised that she'd left them at the beach. Three or four hours had elapsed and we raced there in the car. To our great relief, there they were on a tiny spit of sand with the tide coming in and water already lapping at their feet, but they were still sitting where they had been told to sit. I could have wept and when we got them home, we fussed over them, hugging them, and gave them extra amounts of mackerel pike and rice.

Our imperious cus cus was of course Victoria Rex, who with time had softened her attitude and took proffered fruit from our hands in a ladylike manner. The note attached to her cage was that she was unpredictable and likely to strike.

We received a note from a young lady named Gloria, from up in the Highlands, expressing an interest in our animal collecting procedures. She was a friend of the planters who had been sending animals down to us. She was coming down to Moresby and hoped she could come along with us. We assured her that she would be welcome. She turned up on the day we'd scheduled for a trip and we allset off, with a long, hot drive ahead. She was quite talkative and obviously knew a lot about the Highlands, its people, flora and fauna. She was pretty, aged about twenty-five, a good figure and feminine, but underlying it one could sense a toughness that gave her exploits the element of truth. She had been in some rugged places in mountainous terrain and had accompanied a number of patrols into unexplored regions.

Meeting her reminded me of the time, a good twenty years before, when I was on the *Soochow* trading up in Papua and New Guinea waters, when I too had romanticised about the adventurous life of a Patrol Officer heading into unknown country, meeting tribes that had never seen a white man. Lean, tough men, dressed in khaki, a .38 in a holster, followed by a platoon of police, armed with .303 rifles, and behind them a long line of porters carrying loads on their heads. It was one of the crazy schemes the second mate and I had entertained, like starting a coconut plantation or a chicken farm in Borneo.

On one trip when we berthed in Lae, I met two of them in the pub and we had a yarn while enjoying our cold beers. They certainly were tough blokes, tanned and rugged, and I guess could have been ex-military. When I said I'd like to give being a PO a shot, they shook their heads and were unanimous in saying, 'Don't do it, mate. You'd be mad. It's a bastard of a job!' They talked about gruelling climbs, heat, mosquitos and hostile natives, and urged me to live a comfortable life at sea.

Time was moving on, fast, and we were in a flurry to procure all the animals required by Dr Gordon in Miami, plus the crocodile heads and other heads, now in formalin. It was coming to the end of 1969 and we were scheduled to leave Moresby early in 1970. We'd reached the end of our third term of tropical postings. Time to show the kids a different world.

The cages were ready, forty tea chests, all painted post office red, all numbered and the name of the occupant stencilled in white, plus the scientific name, as required by Miami Zoo. Papuan Agencies, the local customs agent, was aware and alerted to the upcoming shipment, with required airline handling.

I wrote an identical letter to five traders in various districts of Papua: one in Daru, one in Aramia, another in Balimo, and others in Kikori and DarJu.

Dear Sir, I've had a request from my brother in Florida, in conjunction with the Director of the Zoological Division of Crandon Park Zoo, Miami, enquiring into the possibility of getting medium to large size crocodile heads for forensic study purposes, crocs to alligators, skull, skin and teeth structure The request has been put to DASF Konedobu and approval has been granted.

They want a few good specimens, with all teeth intact and have stressed that if any are loose they should be tied, or enclosed with the head. They need the heads with the skin attached rather than the bare skulls. I've been promised the assistance of DASF in fixing the heads in formalin and alcohol, once they arrive here. I would imagine heads from crocs of four to five feet and over would do. Could you possibly assist? The bigger the better.

Because of my brother's association with the Director of the zoo I feel I'm under an obligation to do the very best I can. I'd appreciate it if the costs could be kept to a minimum, and of course reimbursement would be immediate.

As regards sending them to me, the only thing I can suggest is for the heads to be deep-frozen in plastic bags and flown here – marked phone 56520 (home) or 55005 (work), or salted and shipped on coastal vessels. A call on 6280 khz, in or out of Moresby schedule times to alert me would be handy.

I'm also on the lookout for live cus cuses, anteaters, possums, bandicoots, sugar gliders and tree kangaroos. I also appreciate that laws governing the killing of crocodiles and the introduction of permits has caused an exodus of professional hunters, so getting heads may present a problem, especially since the heads need a fair amount of time to be properly soaked.

I'm leaving the Territory on 11/3/'70 and am running out of time. Regards.'

To a Mr Hutton, I added a note.

We're planning to have 3 weeks in India (where I was born) and then on to the UK. All the problems associated with a final departure are cropping up, and as regards the collection we're hoping to get a partial shipment off by mid-January, so that we can concentrate on packing et cetera.

Incidentally, the possum you sent down for Peter, followed by Roger, the striped possum are still here at our place and they've both grown well. Roger gnawed his way through a tea chest so we put him in a stout packing case feeling confident it would hold him. Not so, and it was silly of us to also give him a partially destroyed white ant nest to keep him happy. He made a hole in this and got out in the night. We had a devil of a job catching him (in our bedroom) and then hoovering up fleeing white ants. He sure can bite, right through garden gloves. The packing case now has wire all around it. My wife's recipe for him is weak porridge, milk, honey, a little Bonox, glucodin, prolac high-protein powder all mixed together and he's thriving on it, with of course mangoes and sugar cane. Regards.

All our animals had names and numbered cages to which they were allotted. Information on feeding habits and characteristics was in envelopes, wrapped in plastic and stapled to the chest.

We got to know the animals very well and they responded to the attention we gave them. Some were still semi-wild, some timid, some bold, but in the main we were a happy family. They all had names. Tina and Tim were a couple of sugar gliders, orphans from Lae. They loved their treat of ice cream. George, a male cus cus phalanger from Rigo. Timid. Jill, female forest wallaby: a household pet happy to bounce her way down the corridor. Kenneth, a male forest wallaby. Horace, a cus cus, Jenny, a cus cus gymnotis. Timid. Of course there was our imperious cus cus Victoria Rex, and also Feety. Ed and Fred were male bandicoots, and Peta was a female, all three quite tame eating out of our hands. And we had Alexandra, John, Eugenii, Jane, Gloria, Paul, Cleopatra, Honey, Perri, Sue, Scott, Pepper, Kate, Missy. We loved them all and we were sending them off on an adventure, to a good home. All together, forty animals.

Six large crocodile heads turned up, just in time. They were quickly immersed in formalin and joined the other heads. All set to go. There was a certificate from the officer in charge of the veterinary laboratory stating that the heads of New Guinea indigenous fauna being despatched for scientific study had been treated with 12.5 per cent formalin solution. They were enclosed in plastic bags and wrapped in formalin-soaked cloths inside an airtight metal container: 1 dorcopsulus van heurni (wallaby), 1 phalanger maculatus (cus cus). 3 dendrolagus doriana (tree kangaroos) 1 tachyglossus sp. (echidna), 1 isodon macronus (brindled bandicoot), 1 peronyctes rafrayanus (bandicoot).

Christmas '69 had come and gone. We continued collecting, caging, feeding, vet visits, export papers, antibiotics, paperwork, ensuring all cages were secure and numbered. One tea chest, number one, held all the instructions and feeding details. We were exhausted! We went to bed at three a.m.

The entire shipment was ready to go. Seventeen tea chests and cages, holding forty animals. We were complimented by the Papuan Agency and Qantas officials on the overall compactness and detailed information and paperwork required. Flight details were set for QF282, departing 13 January 1970 to Hong Kong: onward to Los Angeles on PanAm 846 and then LA to Miami on Northwest 42.

With the help of friends who had utilities which would hold cages, and assisted by manual labour from all the house-bois in the neighbourhood, the convoy wound its way to the airport and we saw our friends forklifted into the pressurised holds, tucked neatly together and secured by cargo nets. It was a sad moment as we said goodbye, looking into their bewildered eyes, in a totally different world, away from their green jungle canopies, subjected to the sound of loud voices, of propeller aircraft and the whine of jet engines.

The aircraft made its slow movements down taxi strips, got to the end of the runway, paused, gave full power to the engines and made its run to lift off.

Using the facilities available to me, I phoned a Mr Fong, of Jardines, in Hong Kong, advising him that the shipment was now airborne, that all feeding and other instructions were in cage number one, and to please give all his attention to the welfare of our mob. This he promised to do.

Three days later, we received word from Dr Gordon that the shipment had arrived safely, and he was jubilant. It was a great relief, but tinged with sadness. Our garage was now so empty and there were no expectant faces: no more contented munching on fruit and green shoots, no more tantrums and naughtiness. We missed them, and Annette was sad.

10

There were a few hectic weeks as we packed up and made bookings for our flight to Singapore, for accommodation in Calcutta and then New Delhi. We arranged for our Fiat 125 to be shipped south and stored, and then we had a couple of farewell parties saying goodbye to friends. It was sad saying farewell to Jacob and Naomi, and little Annette: we gave them a bonus of three months' salary. Copious tears were shed as we handed Tramp and Tanya over to Gordon and Pat next door. Nine years in Port Moresby had come to an end.

We flew out in mid-February 1970 to Singapore, then onward to Calcutta. Richard aged seven, Karen five, and Kylie just two, were seeing another world, eyes wide.

Calcutta was a sprawling mass of dirt-smudged, off-white buildings enclosed in a maze of streets and evil-smelling monsoon drains, a leprous odorous sore, buried under the mass of close on ten million struggling, mostly poverty-stricken souls. Buildings of the British Raj and relics of the Empire were impressive, particularly the museum and art gallery, standing magnificently and reflecting an era gone by.

The kids were not impressed with the Indian airline flight to Delhi. The toilet was a hole in the floor between two raised tile foot markers. When they wanted to go, we had to hold them securely to alleviate their fear of falling through.

We arrived at Delhi airport and I was more or less on my home ground, having lived in Old Delhi, just behind St James's Church, a few hundred yards from the Kashmiri Gate which featured prominently in heavy fighting during the Indian Mutiny, street by street taken by the bayonet as British troops stormed through the gate. It was still possible to see where cannonballs had hit the gate and surrounding walls.

We took a taxi from the airport and the driver tried to persuade us into taking tours here and there. He also offered beneficial rates of exchange. After Calcutta, it was good to see relatively clean streets, promoted by the newness of Connaught Circus in New Delhi. Our accommodation at the Central Court Hotel consisted of a large suite of two bedrooms, a large lounge room and a modern European-style bathroom. It all led to a balcony with trailing bougainvillea tendrils. The reception clerk was eager to negotiate prices on travellers cheques.

I used to be a fluent Urdu speaker and I found that the passage of twenty-odd years since 1947 had diminished my vocabulary to some extent, but during our week-long stay I was able to converse with the staff quite comfortably, and they were happy to encourage me. We enjoyed the breakfasts, which were substantial, giving us a good start for the day's activities. Shunning all the usual tours, I took Annette and the kids unerringly to Old Delhi, to 101 Church Street, directly behind St James's Church, where our family lived in one of the North Western Railway houses, my father being loco foreman of the vast repair and maintenance facility. He had been the most senior driver in the NWR, which gave him the reserved privilege of driving the gleaming viceregal train, used only for the viceroy of India, or the special trains owned by the some of the Princely States. Age and deteriorating eyesight, which did not allow him to pass the stringent eye tests, took him off the footplate and a lifetime on the rails. He'd been happy enough, still surrounded by the locomotives he'd driven, as they came in for periodic checks and repairs.

We came to our house, which was exactly as I remembered it, except that there was a double gate blocking the entrance. Looking over it, I was able to see the small bathroom window behind which my sister Sheila would hide. As we rode in on our bicycles, she'd wallop us with a slug from the airgun she was holding. As we dismounted and stormed in, swearing revenge, she would flee to the other end of the house, seeking safety behind my mother. My brother Ed and I were about thirteen or so and Sheila was a bit older.

The fleeting memories ceased as a servant approached and asked us our business. Speaking in Urdu, I told him that this had originally been my home, and he smiled politely, went back to the house and came back with an Indian lady, dressed in a sari. She introduced herself as Mrs Maholtra, wife of the NWR official now living there, and invited us in for coffee. She made a big fuss over the kids, producing small cakes and biscuits. We spent a pleasant hour with her and she was happy to let me show Annette and the kids the room in which Ed and I had slept, and I pointed out the window high up on the wall through which monkeys would poke their heads. I also pointed out the servants' quarters where Abdul, our cook, and Basuk, our bearer, were housed together with the gardener and sweeper. There was also the spare room where we kept our peacock feathers. It was a place with many memories: of quail, partridges, peacocks and peahens, and Bessie, our tame deer.

The Railway Institute building was next door, separated from our house by tennis courts. It was a huge, domed building supported by marble pillars, and the roof area below the dome had cutaways in the walls allowing defensive rifle fire in the case of an assault. Naturally, as boys and armed with airguns, we would play war games and snipe and fire on each other, being careful to aim below the shoulder level. Those .177 slugs used to sting.

I had an eight-millimetre Kodak movie camera and we went over to the iInstitute. I was happily letting the camera run when an Indian army sepoy, with rifle, came up smartly and said that photography was not allowed.

'Tuswirr kheet ceterahnai munnna hai!' He reached out and took my camera.

I protested, telling him that I had lived in the house over there, that we used to play there when I was a kid, and asked what the objection was. He beckoned us to follow him and we were soon surrounded by a bunch of clerical staff who poured out of their offices. The head munshi, behind pebble glasses, said that it was now a military establishment, to which the North Western Railway was attached. I think that there was some paranoia in their collective psyche, afraid of Pakistani spies. He was cordial and accepted that our visit was quite innocent, and gave my camera back to me. In a reflective mood, I accepted the fact that the old days were gone and that change was inevitable.

We continued enjoying the visit and the kids loved the tonga rides. We went to the Red Fort and the Delhi Zoo, and heard the muezzin's call to the faithful at the Jamma Masjid. We rubbed shoulders with the multitude of people surging to and fro through Chandi Chowk, the bazaar of all bazaars. The Chor bazaar or Thieves Market was a revelation: a market for stolen goods. A bicycle stolen today could be found in the market the next day, and bought back for a price.

We booked a first-class compartment for the journey to Saharanpur, where I was born. Our companions in the train were an Indian Army colonel, his wife, and an orderly. The kids were cuddled and we were a happy group with questions going back and forth. The colonel appreciated that I was making a pilgrimage, and showing my family where I grew up, and that we intended going up to Mussoorie to visit the school, Bala Hissar, where I received most of my education. To get there, up to the 6,500-foot level in the Himalayas, we had to go through Dehra Dun to pick up the bus. He wanted to know where we would be staying and as we'd made no arrangements he insisted, despite protests, that we should be his guests at Birpur, just outside Dehra Dun. He was the commandant of the 39th Gurkhas who were stationed there. He said that he had several unoccupied bungalows available and that we'd have an orderly assigned to us, all meals et cetera provided from the officer's mess. The colonel's wife urged us to accept. All we had to do was to present ourselves to the cantonment guardhouse when we'd finished in Saharanpur and got to Dehra Dun.

I took Annette and the kids everywhere when we got to Saharanpur. The station buildings and platform hadn't changed one iota. It was where we stood in late 1947, surrounded by our servants and luggage, waiting to board the train that would take us to Bombay.

We visited the the hospital in the Railway Colony where I was born. Clip-clopping along in a tonga, pointing out houses that belonged to old friends of my parents, to the house in which we lived on Church Street, outside the colony, down the road to the Dhomola River bridge, and the church we went to, where my grandfather was buried.

We stayed for more than a week and then booked seats on the Yatra Transport bus to take us to Dehra Dun. For Annette and the kids, there were scenes of the Indian plains, mustard seed and sugar cane crops, villagers toiling in the fields, and then we were into the low, undulating Siwalik hills, jungle-clad and ideal tiger country, through the Mohan Pass and into the Dehra Dun plain. For me, it was returning to familiar country, giving me a lot of pleasure.

We took a taxi to the Birpur cantonment, right up to the guardhouse and were admitted by a tough, solid Gurkha sergeant with a chest full of medals. He had a clipped moustache and coal-black eyes in a slightly Mongoloid face. He directed the driver to the colonel's house and we were welcomed and made to feel at home. We were allocated a bungalow, fully equipped, formerly officer's quarters, and were very comfortable. Our orderly was Tig Bahadur, a young Gurkha soldier and all our meals were brought across from the officers' mess on trays, with the food in silver dishes. All very splendid. We were invited to visit the officers' mess and it was exactly the same as it would have been when the cantonment had held British regiments. The walls still held the antlered heads of sambah stags, wild boar, black bear, leopard and tiger, with the name of the officer, date and region of its demise. All the work of a skilled taxidermist. There were also glass cases showing stuffed trout and huge sixty pound mahseer. The young Indian officers were extremely polite and as usual the children had their hair ruffled and cheeks stroked.

The colonel mentioned to me, in a private conversation, that his main concern and duty was to raise the spirits of the men under his control and to bring back their confidence. His first action had been to build them a temple where they could find peace within themselves. While on high-altitude patrol, up near the Tibetan border, an area which was under dispute between the Chinese and Indian governments, they had a firefight with a Chinese force and had been badly mauled.

It was not really their fault. They were ill equipped and their clothing was not of the standard needed in that region of snow and freezing winds. The Chinese on the other hand were well clothed, well armed and confident. Gurkha soldiers have a reputation for bravery and for winning and this setback had been bad for their morale.

While in our bungalow, I'd often hear the rattle of rifle and machine gun fire, and the deep cough of two-inch and three-inch mortars. As a schoolboy up in Mussoorie, aged sixteen and above, we were all members of the Auxiliary Force India (AFI) and did marching drills, bayonet and rifle practice, trained once a fortnight by a British army sergeant who was on loan from the army. Twice a year, we had manoeuvres down in the Dehra Dun area, and once a year we had live-round practice on the rifle range, right there at Birpur. It was a full army range with firing positions from one hundred to six hundred yards. We were all assigned a Lee Enfield .303 rifle, which we cherished. To set the sights, we used the 200-yard range and fired ten rounds 'deliberate', breathing easy and slow, squeezing the trigger and making back-sight adjustments. It was lovely to see the bullseye marker coming up. Great memories.

One morning while talking to the colonel, we heard bursts of machine gun fire coming from the range and I mentioned to him that I was familiar with it. Without hesitation, we all got into his staff car and drove towards the sound. There was a detail of soldiers, part of the machine gun squad, and one of them was using the weapon, aiming at a target at three hundred yards. The colonel gave a command, the detail stood back and he invited me to go ahead. I was thrilled and eagerly asked Annette to stand behind me and to set the camera running as I opened up in short bursts. It was lovely to watch the earth erupting behind the targets, plus the noise and the small of cordite and gun oil, the butt against my cheek and the power of the gun under my control.

I couldn't help reflecting on the Delhi Railway Institute episode when my camera had been confiscated for filming in a military area, and here I was at an Indian army base letting rip with a machine gun.

While I was having my moments of fun, Annette was not to be denied. She had mentioned to the colonel and his wife that she was a music teacher and had a few university degrees in the arts. While having tea on our veranda one morning, we were surprised to see a busload of Gurkha troops arrive, disembark and then bring out their musical instruments. It was the regimental band. The staff car drove up and the colonel, his wife, and a couple of officers and their wives joined us on the veranda. We were treated to a concert which started off with the traditional Nepalese anthem, followed by a few marches, such as 'Colonel Bogey', then 'Pomp and Circumstance', finishing with the Indian national anthem. A splendid hour of music featuring bagpipes, bass drums, kettle drums, cor anglais, saxophone and clarinets.

There was more. The colonel's wife took Annette and the children in the staff car to the Dehra Dun bazaar, where there was an abundance of saris and blouses, and Punjabi pyjamas, multi-hued and beautifully crafted. Of course Annette couldn't resist and bought several blouses. They then went to the market, where silver- and goldsmiths practised their trade, a veritable paradise and display of gems set in rings, necklaces, the finest filigree work, and it was there that Annette was able to buy slender silver chains and 'jim jims' which were threaded through the buttonholes. The children were agog with the sight of all this splendour, the sounds and smells, and their dreams came true when they entered the shop of a halwai, where they were served warm purees with a lovely cardamom-scented helping of semolina halva.

I got a pleasant surprise a few days later when an Indian army captain turned up in a jeep, with a couple of sepoys, and a shotgun with ammunition. Under orders from the colonel, he was to take me into the foothills and, using the sepoys as beaters, flush out some jungle fowl. We left the main road, diverted onto some rough terrain and came to a likely spot. The sepoys had hardly started their beating when a couple of jungle fowl broke cover, emitting crackles of alarm and flying low. I followed the leading bird and fired the right barrel and it was a clean kill. The sepoys retrieved it and the captain and I agreed that one bird was enough. The hunt and excitement had provided the right amount of adrenalin. He was a good man and I was happy to hear him talk about conservation. On the way home, we crossed a bubbling mountain stream which was being fished by some sepoys during their off period. The captain called one of them over and after salutes were exchanged he bought half a dozen small fish to take home to his wife. Later, I came to learn that during the Bangladesh war he had distinguished himself and had been awarded the Military Medal.

Two days later, an orderly turned up at our bungalow with a wicker basket, holding a silver platter, covered with a chequered cloth, and presented us a curried jungle fowl with the compliments of the captain and his wife. It was a lovely gesture and the taste of the freshly ground curry masalas in the meat and gravy was unbeatable, beyond description.

Sadly, it was time to leave. We were absolutely indebted to the colonel and his wife. They had been perfect hosts and I don't know why we had been so well treated. They were good people.

We spent a couple of days in Mussoorie. I took Annette and the kids to my old school, introduced myself to the principal and was afforded a good welcome. I showed them the dormitory in which I slept, the position of my bed, took them down to the masters' pantry and confessed my sins, admitting to how we picked the lock and ate the food. Looking across the valleys, I pointed out where we would see deer grazing and pointed out how we frequently saw a couple of leopards relaxing in the middle of our football field, visible in the moonlight.

We finally got back to Delhi to take the next step, the flight to Athens. Karen was ill with Delhi belly, feeling utterly miserable, as were scores of others, all moaning and groaning. Our five weeks in India had come to an end. It was good to show Annette and the kids where I had been born and spent my younger years.

The journey by taxi to Athens from the airport was quite confusing and amusing. Earlier in my life, I'd served as a radio officer on a Greek tanker for a five-and-a-half-year period and had picked up a fair bit of the Greek language, but as I asked questions and responded to the queries of the driver, I found myself talking in a mix of Urdu, having just left India, and mixing it up with Greek vocabulary.

We checked into a medium-priced hotel, negotiating a tariff that included a free breakfast. We did the usual tourist thing, visiting the Acropolis and other sites, including the King George Hotel. During the flight over, we'd made friends with a young Australian doctor and his wife. He was going to do a bit of locum work in Athens and then move on to Switzerland. He booked into the same hotel.

Karen had developed a fever and Kylie was following suit, despite the insertion of children's suppositories, as recommended by a doctor who serviced the hotel. Suppositories, as opposed to injections, appeared to be the favoured method. All three children were now ill and, horror of horrors, seemed to be spotted. The Australian doctor diagnosed chickenpox. We were trapped in Athens for at least ten days.

The manager of the hotel presented us with a bill after a week. I checked and found that he'd charged us for breakfasts even though we'd negotiated a free breakfast deal. We talked about it and he became a bit heated. I wasn't going to waste time, so I went straight to the Tourist Police and gave them the story. I'd heard or read earlier that they were keen to improve the tourist image of the country and they assured me that they'd sort it out. As a matter of fact, they visited the hotel a few hours later and lectured the manager. He was suitably chastised and came to me ringing his hands, saying, 'Why you go to police? We talk, we fix!' Anyhow, the matter was sorted and for the remainder of our stay we got on fine.

Eventually, we left Athens and flew to London. It was good to see my sister again and we settled in to her comfortable home in Banstead, Surrey. Predictably, she made a big fuss over the kids ,who happily romped around her back garden. It was good to just sit, talk and drink endless cups of tea, discussing our family, members of which were scattered worldwide.

Before leaving Port Moresby, we had made an assessment of our finances, our travel plans in central Europe, with eventual return to Australia. We were sorely in need of a good holiday. We found that we'd be able to buy a Dormobile camping van, with enough bunks, cooking facilities and a fridge, so we ordered one from a firm in Folkestone.

We contacted Folkestone from my sister's place and the van was ready for pick-up. Off we went, full of excitement, saw the van, which we named the 'Wombat', test drove her, inspected all the inboard facilities and drove back to Banstead.

A week later, we drove off, heading north, following the Roman road, touring the north, then coming down to Bristol, cutting across and back to Banstead after a three-week absence.

We planned our next stop to be France, Brittany, the Loire valley, staying at various campsites, onwards into Germany, Austria and Switzerland, and eventually to Genoa in Italy, to board the *Galileo Galilei* with the Wombat securely tied down in the hold.

I had feelings of trepidation at the thought of driving on the Continent, on the right-hand side of the road. I bought a small booklet and began reading the road rules.

The time came to say goodbye to my sister and we set off for Dover. I thought I'd be clever and bide my time and drive the Wombat on and up the ramp at the very end, so that when we berthed in Calais, I'd follow the cars off in front of me and follow their example. That didn't happen. When we got to Calais, the ship swung around and went in stern first and I was one of the first to drive off, my heart in my mouth, seeing the big signs saying, 'Tenez à droit. Keep to the right.' I did what was commanded and slowly left the wharf area, with Annette and I both searching for signs that would point us in the direction of Paris. It eluded us and as I looked in the rear-view mirror I saw that cars were successively pulling away, abandoning us to our fate. I turned around carefully and began following them.

By the time we got to the outskirts of Paris, I was beginning to feel quite confident, but when we came to the inner area, I just prayed hard, went around roundabouts, having close shaves and was thankful that the big GB sign on the back was enough of a deterrent for drivers getting too close. We finally got to the huge Bois de Boulogne camping site, stopped at the entry office, checked in and were told to follow a guide on a motorbike who sped away through a maze of tracks, occupied by caravans of many sizes and tents and finally stopped at a vacant site, pointed at it and sped off.

A week at the site was enough, allowing us time to explore the heart of Paris, the Louvre and the Eiffel Tower using the Metro, which was in walking distance.

We then began our vehicular tour of Brittany, then the Loire valley and really began to enjoy ourselves, now quite confident in negotiating French roads. The kids loved hot croissants in the morning.

We dillied and dallied, wandering through the French countryside stopping when a place looked pleasant, preferably with a tumbling stream into which I could immerse a bottle of wine, with string attached, to keep it cool.

At the back of our minds was the constant thought that we were following a subconscious urge to head towards Stuttgart to see our red-winged eclectus parrot, Tosca, and the two whistler ducks, Tony and Tammy. It was imperative that we see them. Six or seven months had elapsed since we had said goodbye.

We eventually got to the zoo and made ourselves known to the manager, and he led us to an elaborate aviary with trees, shrubs and greenery, attached to his house, with several cages in it, and all very natural. We had requested that Tosca be more of a house pet rather than part of a large display, which was disappointing. However, she seemed happy enough. She was resplendent in the company of other parrots When we called, she stopped what she was doing and came crablike along the branch, giving us immediate recognition. The aviary was closed and she came to us as soon as the cage was open. We were telling her what a pretty girl she was, repeating what we'd said to her regularly when she was with us. We stroked her head and down her back, and I was thrilled when I asked her to show me her pretty wings and she gave a little shuffle and held a wing out, allowing me to stroke it, listening to our words of praise.

It was time to leave and it broke our hearts when we went out of the cage, hearing her calling. It still haunts us. Sadly we walked away. We received a bit of a lift when we went to the aquatic area and saw both Tony and Tammy at the edge of a simulated swamp. They were in the company of some other ducks but when we called, they lifted their heads, twisted them towards us and, yes, they came paddling towards us.

We did the obligatory distressing tours of Dachau and Belsen and in a conscious effort to escape we set a course for the cool, mountain air of Switzerland, to stay with friends beside the lake at Zurich.

This chapter of our lives was almost at an end. We set off for Genoa, into the chaotic scenes at the wharf where the *Galileo Galilei* was berthed. We were a small group, totalling just a few hundred paying passengers, the remaining thousand or so being Eastern European migrants, some of whom as we learnt later had little knowledge of the wider world. The crew herded them and treated them like sheep. However, I had the feeling that these people were very lucky, going to Australia, where work was available and where boundless opportunities existed.

For us, it was the end of a journey, heading home. Next stop Fremantle, Melbourne and the sight of Sydney Heads, and the bump of the ship as it came alongside at Circular Quay. Home!

11

We were now in Sydney. This was going to be our home. Between us, Annette and I had done a lot of travelling, all over the world. Now with three children, we were intent on achieving the cherished Australian dream of a house, a garden, a lawn, a car, a dog and facilities in close proximity. Sydney, the 'Big Smoke', with its harbour, the coat hanger bridge and heavy traffic plying to and fro, with a teeming population all around us. After nine years in Papua New Guinea, the change was profound: the tropical island lifestyle was still in our memory banks, and of course the images of the animals we'd known and loved.

I returned to my old position in Sydneyradio at La Perouse, continuing the role I'd known all my working life, using Morse code to communicate with ships at sea and with islands on the Pacific Rim. Despite the fact that I was in the middle of a metropolis, fully engaged, thoughts of my previous years of life in India, of eleven years at sea, were never far away, with images of animals and birdlife, mountains and warm rivers, typhoons in the Pacific and mountainous seas in mid-Atlantic, seagulls and petrels skimming the waves and albatrosses gliding along abeam of the bridge, eyeing us and making us wonder if they carried the souls of seamen like us, and the thrill that came with the sight of seagulls beyond the range of normal vision but if one lay on one's back with binoculars pointed skywards, there, just on the edge of binocular vision, would be specks of white, hundreds of gulls, who having crossed the Atlantic following the wakes of passenger vessels and feeding on their waste, were now returning to the other side carried by the jet stream, a free ride at high speed.

Memories came out of the blue, happenings of many years past. I thought of a ship I was on that had a contract to carry two hundred and fifty thousand tons of iron ore from the Chilean port of Huasco to the USA, and sometimes to Germany. I had become acquainted with an English farmer named Bill Millie in the Vallenar valley who was an amateur ornithologist with an interest in the migratory patterns of birds, as was my brother living in Fort Lauderdale, Florida. He was president of the Florida chapter of the Audubon Society. I became a conduit between the two and began rescuing exhausted birds, way out in mid-ocean, no land in sight.

Little finches of all kinds, even quail, struggling with all their remaining strength to reach us, urged on by us. It was so good to hold a little feathered creature in one's hand and feel the tremor of its heart. Safe. The Greek crew had instructions to bring the birds to me, and I housed them in small cages, giving them water and food. Falcons would settle on the masts and have a free ride. From the bridge, I got the latitude and longitude readings and passed them on to Bill Millie and my brother. When close to land approaching the Panama Canal, I'd release them, happy to see them head for the green, tree-lined coast. Of course Jimmy, my canary, flitted around the cages welcoming the new arrivals. I had bought Jimmy in Baltimore, way back in 1956, and we had spent five years together on a Greek tanker going all over the world but mainly off the South American coasts. He was my faithful companion. I loved that bird and when I signed off I sent him down to Florida, to my brother Arthur.

Old habits and and inclinations came to the fore. My life seemed to be one of contradictions: years of hunting, of holding wounded creatures and then lavishing sympathy and care on them. Life seemed empty without a pet and it wasn't long before we adopted a mynah bird, normally detested by local residents. This was an almost featherless orphan, covered in ants at the base of a tree. Rescued and treated with affection, it became a mischievous member of our family, hopping around, aiming for the sugar bowl. We named her Tricks. A clever and gifted ventriloquist, she was a distant cousin of a yellow-lobed well mynah we had as a pet in distant India. She could imitate the 'tring tring' of a bicycle bell and the voice of the milk vendor with his familiar call of 'Doodh wallah', or the butcher delivering meat, enough to fool my mother, who would go to the door in response. After Tricks had become an adult, we allowed her flight feathers to grow and freedom was offered which was gradually and somewhat reluctantly accepted. However, she was a frequent visitor, clever enough to become a freeloader.

Our next furred friend was a small, unwanted, short-haired puppy. Our neighbours asked us if we could take her. We called her Taffy and gave her to Richard, who was now eleven. They were constant companions and he taught her to pull his billycart.

At work, where I was a supervisor, the workload became too great. Adding to the stress was the heavy vehicular traffic encountered while travelling to and from work, tiring, particularly after a night shift. My colleagues and I had been an elite group up in New Guinea and perhaps I carried this elitism to some degree at this station. Tension headaches began creeping in, sometimes very debilitating. I asked for a transfer and was given Adelaideradio/VIA.

The radio station was located in the Willunga Basin at McLaren Vale on an eighty-acre section with an extensive aerial farm, all of it surrounded by green, verdant rows of vineyards as far as the eye could see. After Sydney, it was a tranquil place. We arrived in December 1975. The Vale was just a village developing into a very small country town. Three or four shops, one hotel, just a main street and a petrol pump: perhaps fifty or so houses, a handful of cars and no banking facilities No shopping centre, just a small store selling basic goods. A large barn-yard structure called 'Fruit Packers' handled all the vineyard and almond orchard requirements.

Accommodation was provided and our house had a large backyard, completely fenced in by corrugated sheeting, butting directly onto a vineyard of dry-grown Grenache. The thought of poultry immediately came to mind and I set about building a simple, secure hen house. During our frequent drives around the Fleurieu Peninsula, we came upon a poultry show at Strathalbyn where the best breeds were exhibited, magnificent cock birds and hens, also ringneck, golden and Amherst pheasants. We bought six point-of-lay hens and, while moving up and down the rows accompanied by the sounds of clucking fowls and crowing cock birds,we saw what I immediately thought was an Indian jungle fowl cock bird,very small and compact with brilliant red colouring, which I'd last seen in the Himalayan foothills. He was accompanied by his plain and brown dappled hen. Annette was drawn to them, naming them Darby and Joan. Of course we had to buy them and were shocked at the price. We were in fact looking at an old English dark-wing, dark-leg fighting cock and his humble wife. Darby's lethal inch and a half spurs were impressive. It was a must: we paid the price. We also bought a ringneck male and two females and a couple of golden pheasants. Our feathered friends were put into cardboard cartons, crowded but comfortable, and driven home. It was a real pleasure to release them into the fowl pen, feeding and watering them. Darby and Joan were given their own pen later.

A day or two later, I learnt what a little terror Darby was. I was walking away from him back to the house when I heard a rustle of feathers and felt a hit on my leg. I turned and there he was, puffed up, crouched, red in the face, ready to launch another attack. I was amused and accepted that it was in his nature. I took a couple of steps towards him but he gave no ground. He won the contest as I walked away but subsequently made sure to watch out when I was in his territory. I made a game of it. I would turn my back and let him rush, then immediately turn and put my foot under his chest and send him flying backwards. He'd land, crouch and have another go. We both enjoyed the game. The tattoo of his spurs against my shoes was part of the enjoyment. I gave the kids a cautionary warning about Darby. Son Richard, now twelve years of age, was quite capable of looking after himself and, like me enjoyed the game, often provoking Darby into action. The girls, Karen ten and Kylie eight, were no match and fell foul of his spurs several times.

Annette continued her academic career and gained her DipT and BEd in music and English. She already had an AMus and TMus diplomas. She began teaching in the local schools.

As a family, we coasted along happily. Cedric, our male ringneck pheasant, was a noble soul with a stately manner as he walked around the yard with his two female companions. It was nice to watch. There was contentment in the camp for quite a while until Darby, who had quietly nurtured his dislike for Cedric, who was bigger and more colourful, decided to make a move towards dominance. He launched an attack on Cedric, spurs flying and dislodging sundry belly feathers. Cedric made no move to retaliate, took the broadside assault and no doubt recorded it as an annoyance

Over a period of time, months in fact, while observing through the kitchen window, I saw Darby trying further provocation, spurring Cedric and strutting off. I had a feeling that the worm would turn. Perhaps it was something hormonal, the approaching breeding season, that triggered a response, and Cedric eventually turned to fight. He spurred Darby with a sudden charge and held him down, pecking him hard. Darby managed to crawl from under and began to run, pursued by Cedric, round and round the yard. I saw Darby slowing down, wings drooping, tripping over himself in total defeat. I ran out of the kitchen, stopped the fight and lifted Darby up and took him to his pen. He lay in the straw, sorry for himself, but I was sure he'd be all right, and no doubt somewhat wiser.

It wasn't long before we acquired a cat, a Siamese sealpoint female whom we named Taganak Tawi Tawi, or Tawi for short. The name always fascinated me. It was a point on the south coast of Borneo, now named Kalimantan. The ship I was on, the *Soochow*, regularly passed it as we moved from Tandjong Priok to Surabaya and Macassar in the Celebes. It was a pleasure to sail in those waters as the sea was calm, sometimes as smooth as glass and when flying fish took off they left ripples that lasted for many minutes. Very different to the turbulent seas off the China coast, heading towards Japan up the Ruykyu Chain.

Tawi was a good cat but unfortunately her sharp claws soon reduced the armrests of our leather couch to a pincushion in appearance, and of course nail cutting was mandatory. However, Annette soon had her trained, and her intelligence showed. She would make a great exaggerated circle around any part of the furniture she wasn't allowed to touch.

Young Richard, now just at the start of teenagehood, found a young puppy, a nondescript mix between a fox terrier and a kelpie. He named her Taffie and they were inseparable. He'd ride around McLaren Vale on his bike with Taffie in a wire basket fixed to his handlebars. He was an enterprising lad and when he had just reached fifteen, he began working part time at the only petrol pump in town, filling petrol tanks, as was the method in those days, accepting cash and giving change, and was eventually entrusted to hold the keys and to close down.

The bane of his existence, when he came home was a young golden pheasant. It was the only survivor out of a clutch of four eggs and grew up immature. It used to behave strangely, totally out of character, and as it grew, it fell in love with Richard, sidling up to him and following him around to the extent that he was highly embarrassed. It was quite comical to see him followed by his feathered friend, lowering a sheath of feathers to cover its face, just leaving space for an eye fixed firmly on the object of its affection, the feathers like a deck of cards displayed in the palm of one's hand, back and forth.

We heard of a situation in the nearby settlement of McLaren Flat where some chihuahua pups were for sale and Annette went there at speed and bought a little female, which we named Ting. She was later mated and produced a girl whom we named Taiyuan. Our house and backyard was running out of space.

Over a period of time, I became acquainted with the seasonal activities in the vineyards. In the dormant winter period, traditional two-bud spur pruning was completed, generally by vineyard owners and local staff, or with contracted teams of Vietnamese teams, all wearing conical straw hats. Machines were developed to do the job faster with sharp-bladed teeth cutting the vines at predetermined height, moving at speed down the vine rows. This method wasn't suitable for bush vines. All the activities culminated of course in the grape harvest, which again advanced from handpicking into buckets into machines which straddled the vine rows with vibrating rods beating the grape-laden vines, dislodging grapes which fell to the floor of the machines and then shuffled into chutes which poured the grapes in a continuous flow into trailers travelling alongside. All fascinating. I frequently stopped my car and talked to the men, gaining knowledge and finally began attending lectures on viticulture given by a prominent winery.

Annette and I had in tandem developed an interest in the activities of the Vale and liked the whole area, a verdant valley, removed from the city. We'd done some adventurous things in our time, were both fit and not afraid of a challenge. We both had good jobs and had made some prudent investments and the idea of owning a plot of land and growing grapes seemed like a challenge we could handle. We asked for advice from friendly vignerons and finally bought a twenty-acre block not far from the radio station, which already had Ximinez dry-grown bush vines, and a similar plot of dry-grown Grenache bush vines. This was way back in 1977. It was satisfying to know that Pirramimma Winery close by would take the grapes. I think they felt sorry for us. It wasn't long before new varieties came on the scene and Pedro vanished. However, Grenache hung on particularly if dry-grown.

What we needed was a bore for water and plans for further planting. Annette was in charge of finances and we slowly moved ahead, driving neighbours mad with our questions and requests for advice. A local water diviner, using a forked apple tree branch and a welding rod as a supplement, found an underground stream, and a bore digger began his drilling and very soon found water at a depth of just fifty feet. A pump was installed, trenches dug, pipes laid, and we were away. Over a period of years, we planted twelve acres of Rhine Riesling and two of Chardonnay. A lot of labour was required: contractors to thump in posts, drip irrigation throughout, straining wires and planting, which Richard and I did, while the girls were tasked with tying down canes and other simple tasks. They let everyone know that they were 'slaves on the vineyard'! Annette of course had her teaching job, and also kept an eye on our costs.

We did more research and decided to build a log cabin home, which came as a kit from Melbourne. It was delivered and built in six months. We left the Commission house and moved into our own home. It was perfect. All up, a nice block of twenty acres gently sloping down to a two-acre stand of river red gums.

I was a shift worker with numerous night shifts on the roster and with all the tasks involved, I wasn't getting much sleep. There were times when I was totally exhausted.

Simultaneously with the vine plantings, we established a lovely garden and I built a row of six cages on a foundation of packed earth and a four-brick-high base wall with posts at intervals, wire all around, roofed and a door to each cage. In it went the chooks, pheasants, a male peacock and four peahens we'd bought, a couple of partridgse and half a dozen quail, and a galah. Our peacock, whom we called Gaylord was magnificent. He'd walk around the veranda admiring himself in the glass, spreading his tail and vibrating it so that it made a rustling sound. The only problem with Gaylord and his girls was that they preferred to fly up to the top of their cages and roost there rather than inside. It was dangerous.

We knew that foxes lived in the swamp nearby and heard them barking every night. One night, one of them was just outside the house, not far from the cages. I woke up and while totally naked grabbed my single-barrel shotgun, fed in a cartridge and silently slipped onto the veranda. He barked and I got closer. It was pitch-black. He barked again and I guessed he was no more than twenty feet away. He barked and I fired at the sound and must have missed him by inches. Being a choke-barrelled shotgun, the charge would have emerged with hundreds of little number six chilled shot as a solid ball with no time to spread as it came out at supersonic speed, whistling past his ears. It must have given him a hell of a fright. It certainly had an effect on Annette because I heard her give a scream in the bedroom. I smiled to myself, disappointed that I'd missed, but relished the smell of gunpowder as I ejected the cartridge.

Daughter Kylie twisted my arm and persuaded me to allocate a small piece of land where she could ride and exercise her horses. She had two, both Appaloosian, Makushla and Zana. Tons of sand were trucked in to set it up. She also had a small white pony named Prince. He had a free run of the place and loved walking on the wrap-around veranda, much the way Gaylord the peacock did. One day, I saw a photograph of him standing in our lounge room, beside the telephone table. Brought in by the kids, no doubt. Quite at home. There was outrage on my part and he was immediately made *persona non grata*. I was a pipe smoker in those days and I found the only deterrent, enough to send him on a different route, was a puff of Erinmore flake in his face, causing him to curl his top lip, sneeze and shake his head violently.

Over a period of months, we lost four peahens then all the quail and partridges when a fox dug under and committed murder. Not a single bird survived. One night when we were watching TV, Annette asked whether I'd heard a funny noise outside. I hadn't but decided to check. It broke my heart to see the vacant spot where Gaylord normally slept. A fox had jumped up, grabbed his long tail and pulled him down. I found Gaylord against a fence where the fox had left him, being unable to pull him through. I tied a white rag to the fence as a marker and was prepared to make a blind of hay bales and to sit up the next night, but my neighbour talked me out of it, saying the fox would smell and sense my presence. He set up two traps (now outlawed), chained to the fence, just near Gaylord's body. The fox came, set off both traps but got caught by one and broke the chain, making off with the trap attached to one of his legs. Not nice.

Not long afterwards, good old Darby passed on, and within a month little Joan followed him. They'd been with us for close on seven years. The pleasure of having animals and birds has to be measured by their loss. Tears flow and I've had no compulsion to withhold my grief, letting tears flow when talking to friends, in the supermarket, on the street, sobbing with abandon. I guess it's a healing process.

We turned the granny flat intended for Eva, Annette's mother, into a B&B, some time after she had regrettably passed on suddenly with an aneurism. Quick and merciful.

We called the B&B Samarkand. Samarkand, a fabled city in Uzbekistan was a resting place and a haven for weary travellers on the famous Silk Route. It still is. We gave weary city dwellers and others from interstate, including their dogs, a quiet spot surrounded by vineyards. Some explored the area, visiting wineries, while others lay back in their reclining chairs and dozed, or spent time in the spa.

I was still brooding over the loss of Gaylord and the others taken by foxes, and I planned to venture down to the swamp area where they had their hide, coupled with the chance to investigate the spot when Annette told me that two of our grandchildren were coming down to stay while she was at a conference in Sydney, adding that I was not to be too harsh with them, and that I should think about keeping them occupied. She further suggested that I should try and catch some yabbies down in the swamp. Hell, I'd never caught one and I guess I wasn't classified to call myself an Aussie until I'd caught some. Simple, they said, just a piece of rotten meat on a string, chuck it in and Bob's your uncle. I went to the local butcher and got a bit of offal and hung it in the shed, letting the flies have a go at it. For a long minute while in the shed, I felt a tightening in my chest, enough for me to make me hang onto a post. There was some pain down my left arm. Taking slow, deep breaths, I went back to house and had a rest. My daughter phoned a few hours later to say the boys were going to see *Harry Potter*, amongst other things, and would not be coming down. Good oh, I could relax.

Early in the evening of the next day, I put the meat in a bucket and with my shotgun I made my way towards the swamp. I detected a couple of wires blocking my way, one of which could have been electric. I dropped the bucket over the wires got down on my belly and, hugging the earth, slid my gun forward and got under the wires. I paused, holding my breath, and again I had a tightening in my chest, stronger and stronger. Jesus! I felt like reaching in and pulling out the almost live thing that was inside me. I put my cheek on the damp earth and sent up a silent prayer, eyes shut, breathing slowly. The discomfort gradually lessened. I lay there letting the sounds of Nature, the buzzing and humming, soothe me. My fertile imagination crept in and I imagined a big brown coiled snake just ahead of me, ready to strike. They'd find my body a few days later. A minute passed and I stood up carefully and surveyed the scene in front. A couple of black ducks came in for a landing, saw me, banked, gained height and rapidly wheeled away.

With a long string attached, I threw the meat in and decided to let five minutes elapse. Wwhen the moment arrived, Id pulled slowly on the string. What a thrill! The first live, brownish-green yabbies I'd ever seen. Six of them, thicker than my thumb, about the length of my hand. They began to scatter and ineptly I tried grabbing them by their tails only to have them flick themselves out of my grip. I found two sticks and managed to hold them that way and consign them to the bucket. I made three more casts and caught seven more.

It was approaching dark when I got home. I put the bucket under a running tap, clearing out the mud. The elation had gone and the thrill of capturing something so wild had a tinge of sadness. I looked down at them, shying away from the fate that awaited them. They were survivors of some of the harshest conditions on earth and I, the omnipotent one, was going to eat them. I know, I'd shot and killed countless creatures in my lifetime, but these little swamp dwellers were something different. I put them in the refrigerator, hoping they'd go to sleep and suffer less. I boiled up a pot of hot water and when it was bubbling fiercely I dropped them in, apologising to each one. That night ,I had my first meal of yabbie meat, vinegar, mayonnaise, a bit of salt and pepper, a small green salad, and a couple of Shiraz.

Annette came home a few days later and I told her about the yabbies. She was pleased but sad for the little creatures, but was alarmed about the chest pains and, without fail, I was to visit the doctor tomorrow. At six a.m. the following day, I got up to make the usual cups of tea and got as far as the kitchen, when my chest was crushed with tremendous force. I couldn't breathe and fell to my knees. Somehow, I crawled back to the bedroom, blurted out, 'Heart attack,' and fell on the bed.

Out of a deep sleep, Annette had to cope with it. I heard her phoning and it seemed like no time at all before the doctor was at my side administering morphine. The ambulance boys came and cupped an oxygen mask on my face. They kept asking me what my pain level was on a scale of one to ten. It was about seven. The tears kept coming as I thought of all the problems Annette would have to face. I was lifted onto a gurney and I asked her to take a photograph as I was carried out and when she protested the ambulance boys urged her to keep me happy. I wanted it for posterity.

The ambulance drove off and through the tinted glass I had a good view of the receding driveway and all the trees I'd planted over the years. I was wondering if I'd ever see it all again. My pain level was about six and I felt quite positive, knowing I was in good hands. A new experience, yabbies, yesterday and a heart attack today. What next? I was just so sorry that this might be my last journey with my life's companion sitting here beside me, holding my hand. I wasn't afraid. What was that poem: 'ready to face that last dim misted trail, when eager eyes and pliant muscles fail, thinking of death as just another place to go, another road to walk, another land to know…'

Long hours of lying in bed, day and night, attached to various probes, became a part of the process of recovery. The blockages in my arteries had been cleared and I was assured that in time the muscle in my heart that had been deprived of blood would soon become a network of barely visible threadlike arteries beginning repair work. I was very conscious of the fact that I had survived a near death experience and began to think of the factors that had allowed it to happen. Too much smoking and grog, beyond the accepted limits. Considering the life I'd led while at sea, with all the excesses, it was a wonder that I'd come this far. I realised I was not invincible and as a responsible husband and father I would have to change my habits.

After several weeks, my heart specialist gave me the all clear and I was allowed out of hospital. I was incredibly tired. We booked into a bed and breakfast down on the south coast. A regular regime of walks on the beach helped lift my spirits, and heart-to-heart talks brought fruition to many proposed well-being projects.

I thought about it hard, steeled myself into facing a challenge and went cold turkey, giving up smoking. After decades of sucking smoke into my lungs and getting the nicotine kick, it was extremely hard, cruel, but I stuck to my guns and fought each urge to a standstill, and won. I waited a while to consider the next move and restrained my urges to reach for the bottle of Shiraz. Again, cruel, a real battle, but in the end I beat the urge. Now I just drink pale ale, 0.5 alcohol content. I feel a lot better for it.

We returned to our twenty-acre property, I as a more reflective person, ready to pick up the strings of life, with Annette and the kids to help.

Quite a number of people were asking if we would agist horses. I had pulled out all the Chardonnay, being unsatisfied with their struggling growth, so there were three acres available. There were no illusions. A lot of work was required but, at a steady measured pace, I felt I could do it. Annette and I talked about it and she gave the go-ahead. There were posts to be pulled out and the three acres were divided and posts realigned. Fencing, stapling, electrification, corrals, watering troughs placed in situ, and three sheds. I took on the challenge and beavered away, slowly, and finally got the job done. The next task was to acquaint myself with horse behaviour, learn the signs and idiosyncrasies of each animal, steering clear of the hind legs and building up trust. The owners of the horses were satisfied and stayed with us for years.

Time waits for no man or beast and inevitably the span of years ran out, and their beloved friend needed to pass on. A friend they'd had for many years. All that love and time together. The rides, the shows. A sad business. I made the arrangements, selecting the site in the gums paddock, having a digger come in and prepare the grave, and having the vet on hand. Ladies shed tears and I put my arms around their shuddering shoulders as the deed was done. No suffering.

Our place was a haven for birds. Magpies in song concerts and of course blackbirds whose renditions were a composition of variables never the same, larks trilling in the sky, reminding me of Jimmy, my canary and fellow voyager. The twittering of starling flocks, hundreds strong, all briefly silent when the gas guns went off. The timed explosions were meant to deter starlings but they are astute birds and would lift off with a whirr, a brown cloud, move a few metres and settle again to feast on the grapes. I found that blasts from the shotgun were more effective.

I was baffled by one particular sound, a sort of croak followed immediately by a thump on the roof. It was quite some time before I realised it was a white-faced heron announcing his arrival, preparatory to moving afield. We had a wrap-around veranda from which one could step onto a gravelled driveway, on the other side of which was a raised garden bed with roses, native hibiscus and other plants. Also a small pond nestled among the bushes, behind which was a green lawn, ending at the base of quince and lemon trees. The trees were flush with fruit, brought on, I think, by the handfuls of rusty nails I'd scattered at their bases. An old slatted bench was at the base of one of the trees, and there, on it, was the heron. We were about thirty metres apart. We observed each other for a minute or two and then I quietly moved into the house. Over a couple of weeks, he moved onto the lawn, taking careful steps as if he was treading on water lilies. He dipped his beak in the pond. He was much closer now to my position behind the glass front door. I don't know why but I decided to call him Banjo, and Annette agreed. She was as fascinated by him as I was, and in fact I felt quite honoured to have received his trust.

I got small pieces of discarded fish from the local shop owner, mainly tommies and Coorong mullet, bits about a finger long. I put a few pieces in front of the bench and a few more closer to the pond. On his next visit, I was thrilled to see him hop down from the bench and cautiously pick up each piece. We were mates now, treating each other with great respect. I could hardly believe it when I saw him leave the lawn area and cross the driveway, getting even closer. The final triumph was when he came onto the wrap-around veranda, right up to the glass door, looking for me. I took a photo which I cherish.

When we sold the property later to our neighbour, a husband and wife team, I asked that they look after Banjo and they readily agreed. A year went by and I enquired about Banjo and was really pleased to hear that he now had a mate and was accompanied by a couple of Banjettes.

The B&B was busy as usual, but we had our quiet times, and then one day we saw some articles on alpacas, stories about them and their gentle natures. We were drawn to them. There was a small paddock near the gums I could use and had enough material for fencing and a small shelter.

I first saw alpacas and llamas when I used to visit a farm in the Vallenar valley in Chile. The iron ore carrier I was on made regular visits to the port of Huasco, which was at the base of the valley. The alpacas I saw were splendid, dignified creatures, heads raised high with an almost haughty expression. I had been befriended by an English couple who had a timber farm in the valley: relatives of P.G. Wodehouse, the English author. They had an adopted daughter named Nena. A romance developed between us. The ship would take a week or more to receive a load of ore, longer if an earthquake ruptured the railway line from the mine. Nena and I would ride our horses past the paddock where the alpacas were corralled. Memories of them still lingered and I felt compelled to acquire a few, and Annette was enthused with the idea.

We observed the procedures and registered our alpaca stud with the association in Melbourne, giving it the named of La Serena. Our first acquisition was a mature pregnant female named Bella, a Huacaya. She was a fierce lady with many moods, sometimes calm and taking pellets from the hand, and at other times she'd have blazing eyes, hissing and spitting a foul-smelling greenish liquid. Everyone knew Bella and her variable moods, but always with affection. She was a good mother, fierce with her protective instincts. Gradually, we acquired more Huacayas, our aim being with careful breeding to reduce the micron level of their fleeces. There were some splendid male sires from Peru and Chile. Peruvian Ruffo and Patagonia Celtic Triumph were notable, with stud fees well over a thousand dollars. Over time, we had seventeen Alpacas, all Huacayas except for one Suri, La Serena Champagne: a lovely fellow. Annette and Champagne had a firm bond and he could be seen walking beside her wherever she went. It was good to watch. After breeding him with all our females, we sold him to a lady in Tasmania. Full of poise, he walked down our driveway and without hesitation went up the ramp into the transport taking him to Melbourne and then on to Hobart. An aristocrat. The lady in Tasmania wrote to us, giving effusive praise for his gentle nature, and said she loved him.

We had some successes at various shows and began to sell regularly, ending up with just nine. At that stage, Annette and I were tired. The B&B was very popular and our occupancy rate had reached 265 nights in the year. We had to hire extra staff to cope. It had been a long haul and it was time to go and put our feet up. We thought about it long and hard. We had no intention of living in suburbia, nor in a retirement village.

We let it be known that the alpacas were for sale and we had numerous enquiries about particular females and it became a cherry picking scenario, whereas we preferred a sale of all nine. We received a frantic call from a Maori lady asking if we had any left and when told we still had nine, she was jubilant and said she'd have the lot unseen. A favourable deal was done. She came about a week later with a whole bunch of Maori lads, strong burly blokes. Sadly we said goodbye to our friends Autumn Angel, Cinnamon, Curly, Misty, little Poco and Snowy as they were put into the van. Then in a feat of energy, strength and determination, fencing staples were removed, fences rolled up, five gates unhinged and then all the pinus posts, a hundred at least, were pulled from the ground, manually with arms wrapped around and a heave ho. I offered them the use of my Massey Ferguson 135 and its hydraulics but they laughingly said no need. All done within an hour by a happy, laughing, joking Maori mob and a very pleased matriarch. A few weeks later, Annette and I visited the property they'd been moved to and they all looked well settle in.

By now our neighbour, David, knew we wanted to sell. He already had an eighty-acre section, plus three twenty-acre blocks, and our twenty would make another complete section. He came over the fence for a chat. He already knew what type of grapes we had, so we showed him our B&B book with the occupancy rate, the spa and gardens all around. We had been toying with the idea of using our place as a wedding venue. We had a chat, agreed on a figure and shook hands, across fence as it were, no agents' fees involved.

Our daughter Kylie lived in an arts-eco village not far away and told us there was a block available. We popped over, saw it and bought it the next day. We would now be in a village of like-minded people, interested in nature, permaculture, self-sufficiency, self-expression and artistic endeavour.

Done and dusted. We'd made a success of our last endeavour, and sadly, yet with anticipation, we drove down to our exit gate, towards a new life.

www.ingramcontent.com/pod-product-compliance
Lightning Source LLC
Chambersburg PA
CBHW050252120526
44590CB00016B/2322